D1590227

An American Legion
Baseball National
Championship Story

AN
INNING
AT A TIME

INKWATER
PRESS

MEL MACHUCA & WILL SHEPHERD

www.inkwaterpress.com

ISBN-13 978-1-59299-553-0
ISBN-10 1-59299-553-5

Publisher: Inkwater Press

Printed in the U.S.A.
All paper is acid free and meets all ANSI standards for archival quality paper.

1 3 5 7 9 10 8 6 4 2

DEDICATIONS

Top of the Inning:

To all of the ordinary American Legion Baseball teams that play in the tournament: you can win it too! That's the reason it's played.

To Our Families: The hope that when your window of opportunity presents itself, you will take full advantage of it.

Bottom of the Inning:

To all the American Legion Baseball players in America who doubt your team's chances to win it all. Don't!

To South Bend Post 50 and all the American Legion Posts that sponsor youth baseball teams: The opportunities you provide and the commitment you make to the development of young people is worthy of your time and effort.

In Memoriam

Dennis Janiszewski, our teammate,

Robert Kouts, our Baseball Chairman and

Woody Miller, a sportswriter and friend who traveled with us

All left us way too early.

Special Thanks

Jeff Kowatch, Editing

Don Steinhilber, Sr., Editing

Todd and Dana Machuca - IT support

Table of Contents

Prologue

*"If you can fill the unforgiving minute
With sixty seconds worth of distance run,
Then yours is the Earth and everything that's in it,
And - which is more - you'll be a Man, my son"*

Rudyard Kipling

The cornerstone of every successful endeavor in sports, business or in life includes this concept. When a window of opportunity presents itself, the clock starts ticking. It's a relentless clock because there's no way to call "time out" and deal with it at your own pace. All you can do is rise to the occasion, or miss it and wait for the next opportunity. Often the most difficult part is recognizing the opportunity before the window closes. Being in the right place at the right time with the right personnel is key.

This is the memory of one such opportunity and how a group of young men evolved into such a formidable force that everyone who experienced it grew from the experience. Everyone who witnessed it could only stand in awe of the accomplishment.

This is about amateur baseball. A game played by so many people in this country that it's taken for granted. Those who play it recreationally understand the basic rules. Those who play competitively try to understand the intricacies of the game. As the level of competition improves; the game itself, so simple in structure, becomes more complex and harder to understand.

What really makes the game so complex is the intangible element, the human element. How do you generate passion, responsibility, and accountability within a group of youngsters, and yet allow them to take ownership of what they need to do to take advantage of the opportunity? You have to convince them that there is a responsibility that goes with being good. That responsibility is simply that you have to play well all of the time. You teach them to take advantage of their abilities and not worry about their limitations. You teach them to break the task down into its smallest component part so that they can see that it's not overwhelming and they can achieve it.

Baseball is a game of statistics and maybe by listing some of ours you may better understand our opportunity and accomplishment:

- **1977 American Legion Baseball National Champions – South Bend Post 50**
- 18 – 0 Overall Tournament Record:
  - State (Indiana) 10 – 0. Sectional, Regional, and State Finals.
  - National- Great Lakes Regional 4 – 0. Six State Champions from the following states: Indiana, Michigan, Ohio, Kentucky, Wisconsin, Illinois, plus a host team.
  - American Legion World Series 4 - 0. Eight National Regional Champions who were State Champions from California, Pennsylvania, Mississippi, Florida, Connecticut, South Dakota, Idaho, and Indiana
- ONLY Indiana National Champion to date.
- Undefeated at all tournament levels
- Defeated the second best team <u>twice</u> at all five levels of the tournament.
- Defeated reigning National Champion and National Runner-Up (1976).
- Outscored our opponents 23 – 4 at the Legion World Series in 4 games.

- In 13 out of 18 Tournament games were tied or behind after 6 innings of play.
- Opponents scored 2 runs – 5 times, 1 run – 6 times, and were shut out 3 times in tournament play.
- 41 – 6 Overall Season Record.
- 25-game winning streak.

Let me add that the team who compiled these statistics had to evolve. We were not the same team at the end of the season that we were at the beginning. How and why we matured into that team is the subject of this treatise. The parallels that can be drawn into business or life experiences, we leave to you.

Pre-game Warm up

Introduction

STRETCHING

This story, <u>An Inning at a Time,</u> was named by the people who lived this adventure. This title was selected at a pre-reunion meeting from a list that represented what we accomplished and somehow described the overriding tenet of the team. An inning at a time is how we approached every game; we played by breaking it down into its smallest component part. This team had the principle characteristics of a successful team. We were fundamentally strong and had an unyielding work ethic. As the year progressed we became focused and strove for excellence.

The program we participated in 1977 was American Legion Baseball, a program designed for 16-18 year-olds. It is a national program that was founded in 1926. It is estimated that more than two million young men have participated in this program. We learned from Mr. George Rulon, National Baseball Chairman for American Legion Baseball, that in 1977 approximately 56% of all active major leaguers had played American Legion Baseball. The sole mission of the men who run this program, led by Mr. Rulon, is to maintain the integrity of the program and to keep its legacy of fair play and good sportsmanship in place.

I consider myself an American Legion Baseball Coach. Why this program? I chose it for several reasons. The first is that once you pick your team and register them, it is yours for the year. This is the team that you will field in the tournament; no add-on players, no substitutions. Second, this program is steeped in fairness and has a governing body that oversees recruiting areas, player recruitment, proof of age, and rule changes at both the State and National tournament levels in order to level the playing field. It even selects the official baseball to be used so that everyone is on the same page. The third and final reason is the tournament structure itself. It is played under Major League Baseball - National League rules; no designated hitter, no speed up rules and no re-entry. The only exception to those rules is the pitching rule which limits a pitcher to twelve innings or three appearances in three calendar days. This last rule is intended as a safety measure to preserve young pitching arms.

Our story will be described for you from the beginning of the year and move through the season as it happened from two different perspectives in each chapter. The *Top of the Inning* is the coach's view, a present tense narration of the events as they occurred. The *Bottom of the Inning written* by Will Shepherd, our second baseman, will provide a retrospective view of the events as seen by a player. You will come to know the team and see how we evolved from a group of teenage baseball players into a National Champion. What we will attempt to describe is what happened and how it happened. Why it happened is the essence of our story.

What I didn't know and what makes this accomplishment so unique was how our talent level compared with that of the teams we would meet as we advanced in the tournament. The teams at the state finals were very strong. At least two of them had Division I pitchers who would have opportunities for significant college careers. The biggest surprise came when we saw the level of talent of the state championship teams from the other states we would play. In the Great Lakes Regional in Chicago, the Arlington Heights, IL team had ten returning players from their '76 National Runner-Up team. Blissfield, Michigan had a pitcher who was in route to the St Louis Cardinals. Kentucky was as strong as the other two teams we played there. At the National Finals the differences were even greater. We would meet with teams that had several draft choices and major Division I players. It also goes without saying that many of them had major-league level pitchers and we didn't. All of them dwarfed us in size. Ergo, the bigger, stronger, and faster comparisons we faced in each level of the tournament.

In comparison, we started the season with two elite players. Bill Schell, our returning shortstop who had played his freshman year at Texas Wesleyan University. The other, Jeff Coker, was being scouted by the Philadelphia Phillies. He would sign with them at the end of our season.

Our supporting cast was also fundamentally strong and intelligent baseball players who complimented our elites. They would prove to be able to answer the bell against anybody we played. Of these, nine players would go on to play baseball in college. Dave Hankins, played in Missouri. Greg Heyde, Dennis Janiszewski, Dave Yates, Jeff Rudasics, Jeff Kowatch, and Dom Romeo in Indiana, with Will Shepherd and Dan Szajko competing at the Division I level in Indiana. Will Shepherd would go on to play at Butler University at the end of the season and Dan Szajko, our only 16-year-old, would go on to Notre Dame a year later and also play in the Montreal Expos organization after that.

Our pitching staff had two workhorses, Greg Heyde and Dave Hankins who would post identical 15 and 1 records and prove to be able to compete with the best pitchers in the country. The rest of our team could stand toe-to-toe with any of the strongest players in the State and, as it turned out, the Nation.

Our role players could fill in whenever and wherever we needed them. We were small, fast and focused, and may have had a greater passion for the game than our opponents, at least when we met them on the field. With these comparisons in mind then, our team, although strong on the local level, was a relatively ordinary team that was able to accomplish the extraordinary. We won the American Legion National Championship.

Having said that, let me add this, you don't win National Championships, they happen to you. You get involved in a program and gather a group of high school players together to play a summer season of baseball. Don't get me wrong, this team had a lot of talent relatively speaking, but I've had other teams with a lot of talent that didn't do what this team did. This team started out as so many of my other teams had, winning nine of the first ten games. Then we took a trip to Indianapolis, where we were promptly handed our heads on a platter. It became evident that we had to go through a complete transformation to accomplish what we did, and that metamorphosis is the subject of this story.

Often in speaking engagements I still get asked, "How do you win a National Championship?" If I knew the answer to that I would have done it again. The only thing I do know is that in order to win it you have to be there and getting there is possibly even harder than winning the final tournament. However, repeating is difficult even if you are able to get back into it. The Santa Monica, California team won the prize in 1976 finished 4th in 1977 and finished 4th in 1978. The Arlington Heights, Illinois team reached the championship game of the finals in 1976 but could not get through the National Regional in 1977.

Our story begins with how we built the team and describes for you how the season unfolded. The early games or Discovery gave us our first look at the team in competition. The Nadir (low point), showed us our weaknesses and the Transformation gave us the time we needed to prepare for tournament play and take advantage of our window of opportunity. It was the relationships which were built as a result of our time together on the road both on and off the field at the State, National Regional and National Final tournaments which were the catalysts. The passion for base-ball each player had was the rest.

INFIELD

Located on the upper west side of South Bend, Indiana is an atypical American Legion Post, and for one very good reason. It contains an old trophy and banner which announces to all who enter that back in the summer of 1977 something pretty special happened to the teenage baseball team that represented this Post, this city, and the people living around it that summer season.

Boys of summer, a common slogan for describing young men and boys who fall head over heels crazy for baseball; playing it, living it, breathing it, consuming all of it. It also is a pretty accurate description of what we were; 16, 17, and 18-year-old baseball players with an emphasis on the "18", what I'm sure we'd all like to be again if the Baseball Gods permitted such time travel and the granting of secret wishes. But they don't. We all have that finite window of opportunity that everyone talks about. It is this window that on a daily basis reminds all of us that we are <u>way</u> past our prime as players, as competitors, and reminds us also that "All glory is fleeting".

Well, we'd like to show you a different kind of window, a window that will give you an inside view to our baseball team's little party that summer. The party of a lifetime. We surely didn't cure cancer, stop domestic abuse, or solve world hunger; nothing that important or serious. We also weren't going to be your cover boys for the next issue of the Fellowship of Christian Athletes Magazine. But what we accomplished as a team, and individuals within a team concept will forever be a part of our consciousness, our approach to things, and our perspectives.

The following descriptions of events and recollections are our exact and sometimes faded memories of that great group of people, that very special team, from that very special summer season. 'Our hope', much the same as Mel's, our coach, in his <u>Letter To The Graduates</u> is that through opening this window for you we will be able to show you a part of us.

Our team found each other again in 2006 after many years away, doing the parent things, the adult things, and the professional things. It's what we're all programmed to do, I guess. We have been together as a team only four times in thirty years since our summer baseball championship season. We came together to attend the Major League World Series in New York City in October about six weeks after our championship. We assembled for our Awards Banquet in December of 1977 during Christmas break, because we all had to rush off immediately after winning the National Championship to our respective colleges, high schools, and jobs. We also got together for a twenty-year Reunion Game against the then current team at Post 50 in 1997, but our entire team couldn't make it as some players had migrated to other parts of the country by then and had job and family responsibilities that prevented their participation. And we came together most recently for a 30th reunion in 2007. We played golf, had a banquet at Post 50, and were recognized at Coveleski Stadium in South Bend before a minor league game.

This is a story about highly competitive youth baseball, and thus needs to be mostly in the language of baseball, with all its imperfections and liberties. You'll have to allow the sentence fragments and phrases. It's how most baseball people think, talk, and communicate. Baseball people will understand it. We have no doubt about that. We want all of you to be there with us though, so you can feel what we felt, see what we saw, experience what we went through, thus taking the journey with us. I hope we succeed in that mission.

The Prologue lists most of what our team is known for spanning that summer. Our legacy. Our team accomplishments. We're very proud of them. We earned them against the best of the best, for our age group, in these United States of America. In the end, there was no one left to play.

An Inning at a Time

1ˢᵀ INNING

The Making of a Team

"Anticipation"

TOP OF THE 1ˢᵀ

Coaching and managing a baseball team is more about managing people than it is about the game. The first and most important goal of playing this game is to have fun. The best way to have fun with it is to love it and be good at it. I probably have more fun with this game than most people, because I love it! The game is simple; the people who play it are complex.

Teenagers by definition are in a very complicated part of their life, half child and half adult. Teaching, leading and motivating them as any parent will tell you, is at best tricky and often times difficult. In retrospect I think that my advantage at this point is that I have only been a parent for seven years and consequently haven't had to deal with a teenager of my own yet. I could treat these players as peers even though I am clearly older than they are.

In addition to the players, there are other important people who are part of this program. Two of these are Bill Barcome, my assistant coach and Bob Kouts, Baseball Chairman for Post 50.

Let's start with Bill Barcome, who has worked with me for the past two years and has made a total commitment to the program. Bill looks to me as his mentor and absorbs everything I tell him. Although he supports me in all aspects of the program, he still offers suggestions and asks questions about my decisions. He volunteers for everything and has built his own baseball philosophy about working with this team. I give him total responsibility for coaching first base and he accepts it fully realizing that I am running the game from my spot in the third base coach's box.

Bill's personality adds a unique perspective to the team's culture with a positive result of softening the sometimes stressful nature of the highs and lows a baseball season can take. Just talking with him after games allows me to relax and reexamine what has happened. He gives me a second pair of eyes and presents a different point of view that I have grown to appreciate. The players sometimes say things to him they wouldn't say to me. Their reaction to his often times witty comments puts the importance of the game in perspective.

The sports writers and public are giving me credit as the driving force behind Post 50's baseball program and maybe on the field I am, but the real heart and soul of the organization and the man who was keeping it alive waiting for me to get here is the Post 50 Baseball Chairman. He has held that position for nearly twenty years. His name is Bob Kouts. A true Legionaire; he stands five feet ten about 260 pounds, flat feet and a heart as big as any you'll ever find. He doesn't love baseball; he loves American Legion Baseball. In his life he loves his wife, Edith, the most, followed by his children and then comes the American Legion and then American Legion Baseball. He likes cigars and drinking beer but only at the American Legion. He has held every elected position at the post; has been commander several times and decided that he would be the baseball chairman or overseer for it for the rest of his life.

The day I walked into Post 50, changed his life forever. Bob has always raised enough money for the program by himself. He sells 50-50's, raffle tickets and deck's of cards at the Post but he is always open to new ideas. When we expanded the program we needed more money. Unhesitatingly he accommodated us. Another change is in his view of how he fits into the state American Legion baseball program. It isn't because of me but because of the success of our program. I should say *his* program. He only loaned it to me. His sole direction to me when he agreed to let me coach the team was "I don't care who you beat as long as you beat Post 357 (Our cross town rival)".

Bob has a strong sense of fair play about him. He is very noble about the American Legion in general and the baseball program in particular. It isn't about winning or losing; it's about participating. To prove that, you need only examine his record; he has lived through many coaches over the years. Some who coached also experienced great success in their own high school baseball programs.

In order to be successful, players on teams need to build relationships with their teammates, but building relationships takes time and our season is only eight weeks long. The question then is can this happen in so short a period of time? I hope so. I know that relationships have four parts, trust, reciprocity, empathy and bonding. Trust is the initial component that must be conveyed for the rest to occur. I have to begin working on it from day one.

It's May 1977, the Saturday before Memorial Day, and I am somewhat impatiently waiting for the high school tournament to progress to the point where the schools from which I'm drawing are eliminated so that I can begin putting my season together. Let me explain. The high school baseball tournament in Indiana is like the basketball tournament, a single elimination free for all with only one ultimate winner. Every school participates and plays as long as it keeps winning. One loss sends you home and the summer seasons officially begin.

The phone is ringing; I'm sitting in the kitchen of our home drinking a cup of coffee with my wife, Lynda. It's Bill Schell, last year's starting shortstop, who has just completed his freshman year at Texas Wesleyan University. "Hey Bill, how was your year?" I ask. "It's Billy Schell, Hon," I tell my wife. I'm hoping that he wants to come over to visit. Bill has just completed a seventy-two game spring season, with the twenty-five he played last fall, he has played ninety-seven games since the last time he played for me.

I'm procrastinating about cutting the grass which I know is my job. I already put it off for two days. It's very green and long and beginning to blow in the wind reminiscent of a wheat field near harvest time. Todd, although big for his age, isn't big enough to mow the lawn yet. I can't even delegate it to anyone.

If this were a baseball diamond, I wouldn't have hesitated at all but it isn't, it's just my yard. I love baseball. I have played it as long as I can remember and have played on organized teams since I was nine years old and in some years on two or three different teams at a time. This past April, I turned thirty-three and my role had changed from player to coach several years before. I can't stay away from baseball. I have to be part of it. At this point, I have already coached for three years in American Legion baseball. This level of play involves players who won't reach their nineteenth birthday before August 1.

Bill starts with "Coach, I haven't played baseball in five days and I'm starting to go into withdrawal." Bill continues…"We need to have a practice right away!" "Who can you call?"

Bill Schell is a given! Bill has baseball exuding from his pores. He looks like baseball, he feels like baseball and he smells like baseball. Isn't there an old saying, "If it looks like a duck…"? Schell played with us in 1976 but when he returns this year ('77) after a year at Texas Wesleyen, I know that he'll bring even more credibility to the program. I also know that he is about to become the anchor of our team. My problem becomes who can I put around him that can play up to his level? We have some very talented people returning with him but he's our drawing card for other players that we need.

The most important part of baseball to Bill is the practice or game going on at that moment. He doesn't worry about yesterday's game, it's gone. He doesn't worry about tomorrow's game, it's not here yet. His only concern is the game he's playing right now. To take it a step further, he feels the same when he's batting or fielding a ball. His fundamentals are impeccable, his appetite for baseball voracious, but the irony is that he is as patient with those around him as anyone I've ever coached.

Although he was the fastest runner on the team and a .500 hitter last year, I never gave Bill the green light at bat or on the bases. He always follows my direction. I did empower him on defense. Positioning, relays, cutoffs and double plays are his to control and as the team leader, he does. He defined his role on the field and he defined his role with me and furthermore he defined my role with him. I led him because he let me lead because he knew that this game needs total communication. None of that will change this year. Everyone has to know what everyone else on the team is doing.

Psychologically, Bill gets it! Even recognizing the difference in his level of play from the other players on the team; he never puts them in the pejorative. He understands the game and the reason for playing each and every play. He also knows that when you're as good as he is, a responsibility goes with it. Bill knows that he has to play well all of the time. He also understands that as our shortstop he is limited to that position and he can't simultaneously cover the other eight positions. He was and is our All American shortstop and is fully aware that no matter how much he expands his coverage of that position or how well he plays, he still has to depend on the rest of the team members to do their parts. On offense, he knows he will only bat one out of every nine times and is guaranteed to leadoff only once per game. The people who follow him in the order have to make up the difference and he really helps by leading by example and by teaching them some of the things he knows. On base, he makes so much happen that it makes it easier on those behind him because pitchers have to worry about him all of the time. They can't concentrate on the next hitter. Most importantly, Bill sees the entire field all of the time, not many players can.

"Bill, I can call Mike, Will, Marc and ask them to bring somebody with them; you call some of the Clay guys and tell them to do the same. That should give us enough to have some semblance of a practice. I'll meet you at Boland at 6 tonight and try to get Boland Park for 6 tomorrow, okay?"

Now I urgently need to see who is going to make up the team that I will put around Bill to create the team that I want to build.

Bill is a superstar at this level, but the real measure of a superstar is not only how well he plays but how the players around him perform.

I feel good after that conversation because it means my season will start sooner than planned. I start calling people and everybody I call agrees to be there. A lot of that has to do with the success we had last year. We won the sectional and weren't eliminated until the second round of the State Regional in Kokomo.

With a practice scheduled today and one for tomorrow, I decide to remove all obstacles and the lawn is one of the main ones, so I cut it. This will become my first on the field look at what kind of a team we might have this year. Although the Adams and Clay contingents are still alive in the tournament, we have the returning players, LaVille and Marian High Schools and some kids I invited who sat out their junior or senior high school year at Clay High School. Overall this is not a bad group with which to start. We are now on our way.

LaVille High School has sent me two players a year for the past two years but this will be the third year for Will Shepherd. In American Legion baseball in South Bend, you usually only get a player for one year because of the intensity of the high school programs. Now and again you get a seventeen-year-old high school graduate who is eligible for two years. Very few and far between are three-year players. These are the players who were good enough at sixteen to make your team and committed enough to stick around for all three years. Will is one of the latter because he is a three-year player who found a place that he identifies as playing the level of baseball that he needs to play.

Will plays the game with all of the power he has, muscle and brain. He analyzes the game both offensively and defensively and in this his third year, he comes to South Bend to win a championship, any championship, he can smell it. He is not only innately intelligent but also insightful about everything he does on the field and what his opponents do on the field. He comes to me as a pitcher/ shortstop but will start out this year as a pitcher /

outfielder. I trust that he will complete the season as a mainstay, shoring up our infield or our outfield, wherever I need him.

Shepherd analyzes everything about every game he plays. I will bat him this year at cleanup, fifth or sixth depending on who else we get to play for us. It doesn't matter where he is in the line up, he'll know what is happening on every pitch. He is keenly aware of the benefit of facing pitchers who always seem to be pitching to him from the stretch because we always seem to have some-body on base when he comes to bat. He accepts my direction, but always has to rationalize it in his mind. Never does he not totally think about what I direct and why I make a particular decision. He thinks about situations, who he follows in the batting order and who follows him and why. Defensively he is equally capable of playing in the outfield or the infield.

Also returning from last year is Mike Clarke a centerfielder / pitcher from Adams High School and most recently from Indiana University. He throws right, bats right and has good speed. Mike has a strong arm with great instincts both offensively and defen-sively. His head is always in the game and he's a fundamentally sound player. I initially think he is going to be a standout pitcher and the anchor of our pitching staff, but an injury to his shoulder might keep that from happening. I liked his pitching form as soon as I saw him last year. He has a fastball, an overhand curve, and a changeup that makes him hard to hit. Offensively, he's a solid con-tact hitter; he makes things happen when he comes up with men on base. He's deceptively fast on the base path and in the outfield, maybe because he always gets a great jump on the ball. As a cen-terfielder, everything hit to center is a can of corn. Mike is the boy next door-- clean cut, blonde hair, blue eyes, good looking. He is six feet tall, 170 pounds and always has a smile on his face. Confident in his abilities, he knows his position and is always ready to play it. He is singularly the most unselfish player I ever coached.

Another returning player is Mark Toles. He can fit in wherever I need him without hesitation or question. This is Mark's second year and he knows my coaching style and what I expect from him.

His move to first came as a result of the number of middle infielders we have. I am totally comfortable with him on the field but he knows he's going to have to give me his best baseball in another position in order to play every game. He's 6 feet 2 inches tall, slim built and is used to playing shortstop, but accepted the position change to first base with enthusiasm. This is a key switch because he isn't used to playing the game from that side of the infield. His knowledge of baseball is insightful but the most important part of Marc is his hunger to play the game. He always plays under control and that coupled with his passion, makes him as asset to the team.

The last of the group who are returning is Gary Vargyas who played second base for us last year. His primary sport is football and he is on his way to play at Purdue University. He was a linebacker on his high school state championship football team and played very aggressively. In baseball, defensively he has limited range but his enthusiasm makes up for it. He brings what I call controlled toughness to our program. His primary concentration is on hitting. He is a good contact hitter and hustles all of the time. He is also a spark plug and has the ability to fire things up when they start to get too quiet. I see him as a team player open to coaching.

Bill and I arrive at Boland Park about 5 P.M. It's Sunday afternoon and we're the only ones here. Starting time is six so we have time to put the bases out and rake the batters' boxes and pitcher's mound if needed. I asked Bob Kouts to arrive around 7:30 with the baseball forms we need. He always likes that part and wants to be included.

There are ten guys who show up at our impromptu practice. As they move onto the field, they seem loose but I can tell that they're checking each other out, measuring their competition. After a while they appear to be chomping at the bit because they see some of the talent we're starting out with. After they warm up, I hit infield and outfield. They're throwing hard and pushing to make a strong impression on each other. After getting a first look at the way they field the ball, it seems as though we are in midseason. This marks the beginning of daily practice sessions for the players and daily planning sessions for the coaches. The best part of this is that we still don't have the whole team.

The drawing card for new players is our returning players. We are starting with this five-player nucleus from a team that won the sectional tournament last year and had posted an overall record of 28 wins and 12 losses. Along with our returning players, we have put together an impressive list of candidates to fill out our roster. The other thirteen will be first-year players who have to believe that they want to be part of this baseball program. They also have to know they can actually play the game and have fun doing it. There is nothing promised here for their participation. American Legion Baseball is sort of a last hurrah for some because they instinctively suspect this is the highest level they will ever play.

This first week of June will be a long one as we wait for our other players to appear. Bill Barcome and I, armed with our list of anticipated players attend the high school tournament games. We create a list every year and yet the actual team that we field is always slightly different from our list. We immediately have to modify our list when a couple of people enroll in service academies and will not be joining us. Another is signed by a pro team. So we roll with the punches and here we are ready to run a tryout to begin building the 1977 edition of American Legion Post 50 Baseball.

This week, the only thing we can do is wait to see which teams will lose and end their seasons and which teams will advance. As each team is eliminated, I call some players, while Bill Barcome calls others. We know we have the La Ville players because Will Shepherd will bring them. Jeff Coker is a third baseman for Adams High School. He is a power hitter without peer in the area, everyone knows he will eventually be signed by a major league team and most are surprised that it hasn't happened yet. For now it appears that we have the left side of the infield set. Our task then is to find people who we can play around Schell and Coker.

The other invited newcomers are from the updated list Bill Barcome and I have had to revise. From Adams High School, our base school, we get Coker and a second baseman, named Jim

Andert. I like Jim's mechanics at second and on the base path. From Clay High we get three varsity pitchers. Dave Hankins, who will pitch in the North- South All Star game and Dennis Janiszewski who was named but didn't play because of a broken finger, are the first two. The third pitcher is Jeff Rudasics who throws in the low eighties. I don't know a lot about him, but I'm glad he's here. Along with them I have Scott Madey, a catcher with a knee history and John Ross, who caught in the younger Clay programs. These two are important to us because no other school has a graduating senior catcher. Rounding out our pitching prospects are Dave Yates a giant 6'5" right handed heater from Marian High School and Jeff Kowatch a very normal sized right hander from LaVIlle High School with three years of varsity pitching experience.

We make it a habit to concentrate on graduating seniors and coaches' recommendations because most of the high schools have mandatory summer programs. Our returning players are a center fielder, three shortstops and one second baseman. We have some changes to make and a lot of new people to look at to decide what their roles will be.

By the end of the week, all of the teams within our recruiting limitations have been eliminated from the high school tournament. On Saturday we have our first real tryout day at Boland Park. Those ten plus all of the recruits are here. They seem as anxious as I am to see who has shown up. After they arrive at the field, I can sense some hesitancy about how they should act in front of the other players or the coaches. I can see in their faces a question of "...how will I fit in here".

The year starts literally with fourteen players, 2 catchers 8 infielders, 1 outfielder, 3 (only) Pitchers; four of the other-position people are varsity pitchers in high school. Our total pitching staff is seven and although that's very positive, we don't have a lefthander in the group. There is another new player who shows up at tryouts and he is also a pitcher who is our fifteenth player. He'll move our count up to eight pitchers with tournament experience; his name is Greg Heyde. At first glance, this initial group makes it appear that we're only short on outfielders. In point of fact we have too many infielders; only one for sure catcher but are very strong in pitching. Even though we see this, we have to start working with what we have because the season is only a week away. We have a lot of talent but nobody knows where they stand in respect to positions on the field or in the batting order. Suddenly every one realizes they'll have to earn their spots.

BOTTOM OF THE 1ST

Trying to get a sense of what our team could become was exciting for me as we prepared for our season because I had played the previous two summers on the Post 50 team and knew who we had coming back, and I also was eagerly awaiting some of our new guys. I knew they would add a lot to our team. I was especially looking forward to playing behind the pitchers that were going to compete for us. They were strong and had distinctly different styles, motions, and personalities, which I thought would give our opponents lots of problems. As it turned out, I was right about the pitching.

I had unsuccessfully tried to talk two other players and class-mates of mine into coming out for our team. Jeff Kowatch was coming with me. It took some convincing but I assured him that we had a chance to become a great team and that he needed to be a part of it. I had no idea in early June how important Jeff would become to our development as a championship team. For both of us, we would have to compete for our jobs and playing time. It was not as new to me because I had played behind guys from South Bend the previous two summer seasons. But coming from a much smaller school than the other players, we were used to playing a lot and starting, and being the playmakers for our high school teams in different sports, including baseball for three years.

A fact that is still inconceivable to me is that not one player on our championship team was a part of a sectional championship that spring in baseball. All four teams that made up our American Legion Team were defeated in the first phase of our high school state tournament. That's a true testament to the talent level of our area. We had five players returning from the previous team and it was a good mix of players; Mike Clarke, Bill Schell, Marc Toles, Gary Vargyas, and me. Three of those guys had completed their freshmen years at college. Marc Toles and I had just graduated from high school in May.

Mike was a very good versatile player, who could help us in many ways. He was a top flight pitcher with an assortment of pitches, plenty of big game experience, and moxy. He also was an outstanding center fielder and hitter. Bill was clearly the best player on the field as our shortstop. Gary, or "V" as we called him, was a linebacker at heart always, but what he gave us was a true competitive spirit at second base and his personality and leadership were perfect for our team. Marc was a middle infielder like me and we were both just looking for a place to play to get involved. We had played behind people the year before and were looking for a break of some kind. I'm speaking for Marc here also but I believe both of us knew that we would have to play different positions to get playing time, at least at the start of the year.

So we assembled a solid, although not large, returning nucleus mixed with some incoming proven talent that gave our coach something to work with as he looked at the possibilities for this year's version of the Post 50 team. Who exactly would be added? At what positions? I was hoping the Clay guys that I knew of would want to play, especially the two pitchers who had led them for two full seasons, Dennis Janiszewski and Dave Hankins. They had both pitched in big games and were battle tested in high pressure tournament atmospheres. Clay had many talented players and everyone knew we could be helped with their contributions. I learned at some point before we began tryouts that a couple of guys from Clay committed to Service Academies and another player was drafted out of high school. It did not overly concern me though because I still felt we could pick up some serious talent.

Jim Andert and Jeff Coker came from Adams High School. To me, they were a complete unknown (Andert) and a confirmed RBI factory (Coker). I knew of Coker's prowess at the plate. I knew nothing of Andert, though. I found out very early on they both were named to the All-NIC Team and that told me a lot. The Northern Indiana Conference was an outstanding conference during our years of high school baseball. To be named to that group meant you were putting up some real numbers and making some plays on a consistent basis. There was no doubt in my mind they were very good players.

From Marian, I had really no clue as to who Mel might want for our team. Even though I played against them in our high school season, I was only familiar with a couple of guys, and one of them was too old to play again with us. My experiences with Marian baseball had not been so pleasant on the high school level.

As a junior, Marian had defeated our high school team at our place on a super cold and windy day in early April when we had faced a skinny, short, hard-throwing pitcher who just totally shut us down with his fast ball. I remember it vividly because of two things; one, he never gave me a pitch to hit in any of my at bats. And two, he was really competitive and nasty. He made an impression to be sure. I knew his name, Greg Heyde, and I knew he was also a standout wrestler. I assumed I would never see him pitch again because he had graduated the year before me. The summer before he had not pitched for us at Post 50 and I did not know why.

What was Mel's plan for us? Who would actually come to play for us? Would we have any chemistry? I had played on two Post 50 teams before, and we were always missing that key ingredient of TEAM. I could tell that Mel sensed from these first two teams that we were missing something very important and fundamental in our approach. We seemed fragmented, cliquish, with those teams. Talent certainly wasn't the problem, different agendas were, though. I wanted this team to be different in that sense.

I wanted to win a state championship, period. I believed before we even assembled that summer that if we could attract the right people from the four high schools, along with our returnees, we could compete for a state title. The summer before, we had defeated our rival, Post 357 (the reigning state champion) in the sectional, but lost in the regional round at Kokomo. That gave us a first taste. Now the challenge for Mel, and for us, was to take it another full step. No regrets. No shoulda, coulda, woulda's.

As the only 3-year player on the roster, I felt that somehow I must provide some form of leadership to this group. Exactly how I wasn't sure in the beginning, but I felt some responsibility at least on some level. Mel would provide the real key ingredients for leadership, he always did. As for the rest of us, I hoped we would develop leaders as we went along.

How coaches blend talent together is interesting. Some coaches choke when surrounded by many very good players. They are overwhelmed, and let the inmates run the asylum. Some micro-manage and drive everyone crazy. From the beginning I knew Mel would find the right lineup, the right pitching rotations, the x's and o's so to speak. Mel could sense that this group had a shot at being pretty successful. I was really interested in how he would go about molding our group together, both athletically as a baseball team, and as teammates, hopefully all pulling the same direction on the rope.

The making of a team is not as easy as most armchair QB's think. You don't just roll the balls and bats out and say "let's play ball", especially with teenagers. We all came from different places; geographically, emotionally, mentally and physically, as well as our baseball and school backgrounds. It takes great planning, execution, and preparation. That's where the coaching leadership really makes a difference. How do you set up the potential of a team, keeping in mind all the strengths and weaknesses, to get the most out of the entire group? How do you recognize opportunities to push, teach, and communicate with players from a coach's perspective, and from a teammate's? This is the real nuts and bolts of "making a team". Personalities can be as different as stars in the sky. Will they respond? Can they understand what you're trying to do?

I don't remember ever meeting or even seeing Dennis Janiszewski, who people called Jano, before the first practices for Post 50. I knew of his success and reputation, though. I was really surprised to meet him in person. I had in my mind thought of a big strapping guy who intimidated opponents with power and persona. Instead, I met a fun-loving, perceptive, intuitive, little, thinking man's pitcher who used craft and guile to compete with and frustrate opponents. His physical presence or lack there of, made me curious and was at the same time confusing to me. He certainly didn't overly impress me in the beginning. And yet, his success for Clay the last two years was to say the least, impressive. Was this the kind of pitcher we were pinning our hopes on?

I had faced Dave Hankins in a game at Clay Park my senior year and had somewhat figured him out while he was warming up in the bull pen. He, like Jano, had an excellent resume over his three-year career, and was clearly a pitcher who could win for us. I tried to tell my high school teammates in that game that what you had to do against his slider was move your stance in very close to the plate and his outside corner dominance would be negated. He had excellent control of the strike zone. My adjustment worked well against him, but my teammates were a little hesitant to stand on the inside corner. Bottom line, we were defeated again...by the Colonials. I was anxious to have him as a teammate though, that I remember for sure.

I had absolutely no clue about Jeff Rudacis, Scott Madey, and John Ross. They were all from Clay but I didn't know anything about them and had no memory of playing against them in our annual DH's with Clay. Another unknown to me was Dave Yates from Marian.

In essence, I knew very little about this team in the beginning, even less about this group than the two previous ones. I was satisfied and confident to let the coach make the decisions about who should join us. Honestly, I was just hoping my friend and high school teammate, Jeff Kowatch, would make this team. That isn't a knock at Jeff's talent. But he's not one of those guys that jump out at you in a tryout atmosphere. He doesn't hit the ball 400 ft. or throw the ball 93 mph. He's the kind of player that just beats you, and does all the little things that are so very important for consistent success on a baseball field. I knew his game and what it would add to our team. But he was a relative unknown to Mel and the guys. He would have to prove himself.

It was unknown and yet I had a ton of confidence that we would somehow collect the needed pieces to be successful. Marian, LaVille, Clay, and Adams, add up to some pretty good players. The most important question on my mind as we assembled in the beginning was whether these guys wanted to win as badly as I did? It's all I really cared about. I just wanted to win. But everyone does, don't they? The anticipation of my final season at Post 50 was incredible. I couldn't wait. For me, it was not so much WHO but HOW. What kind of team would we and could we eventually become? I anxiously awaited the phone call from Mel that I knew was coming shortly.

2ND INNING

The Discovery

"New Beginnings"

TOP OF THE 2ND

Our "tryout", as we call it, isn't really that. Our "tryout" is really our chance to see if the people we have invited actually show up and it is our first opportunity to see what our talent spread is. We recruit the team, with a main goal of beating our rival team in South Bend. Locally, every team knows all the talent on each team, and each team figures themselves as the favorite, especially in the first level of the tournament. Most media and coaches think that the perennial teams will prevail. In years past they always have.

We know about the five players who are returning and where they were at the end of last year. We have invited an additional thirteen, who we think will fit in with this team. Not all of them are available. What we have to see is how the newcomers will match up against our returning personnel. We can carry eighteen on the roster and I know that some additional people will show, but I really don't want to have too many there. The more you have the harder it is to measure their skills and attitudes.

Historically, I split the season into three parts. The practices plus the first ten games are the *Discovery* portion. The out-of-town trip and/or our midseason tournament are the second part. This part, out of necessity, falls in and around the 4th of July plus the next six games. The third part of the season begins after we make corrections in positioning and personnel and is made up of the last ten games of our original 40 game schedule. It's here that we attempt to identify our best lineup and prepare for the sectional tournament.

The Discovery portion of the season is my chance to measure the skills of the players that I have selected for this year's team. I have time to observe each player's strengths and identify what he needs to work on in basic fundamentals. Let me say now that no matter how talented your players are, they can always get better. John Wooden was asked one time how he could recognize a super-star versus just a very talented player. His response was that the way to recognize whether a player is a superstar was to see how he affects the play of those players around him. The closest thing we have to a superstar is Bill Schell. He played shortstop in high school and Legion ball, and even though he plays 2nd base in college I need him to play shortstop again; he agrees.

Our players come from the four different high schools and only know each other from games they have played as adversaries or from newspaper articles during the season. The thoughts about playing for this team from their high school coaches were mixed. The jury is still out as to whether we run a good program or not. Most agree to send us their graduating seniors because there simply is nowhere else for them to go.

Another unanswered question is in the minds of their fathers, since I had moved in from Indianapolis only two years before, they don't know anything about me either.

What the players seem to accept is that politics will play no role in their selection to this team. They also understand that this is the next level of competition. We have graduated seniors and some college players. They also know that they will have a chance to show me what they can do on the field but they also know they can't rest on their high school reputations because they don't know if I know who they are. This is a whole new ball game. Understanding the level of our returning players by reputation, they want to be part of it. The returning players are ahead in that regard. They, at least, had the previous summer they experienced as teammates playing for me.

The newcomers can only see this tryout as a new beginning; something that they have not experienced in a long time. Having said that, this year's team appears to have personalities that are so diverse that an outsider wouldn't know if they can ever function as a team, let alone become efficient. Their high school experiences are different because their coaches approached coaching differently. The saving grace, however, is that their high school coaches, Lenny Buczkowski, Jim Reinbold, Ben Krasiak and Dale Cox all run programs that emphasize strong fundamentals.

My advantage comes from the fact that I'm not their parent or a school teacher or a high school coach. I can actually approach this group from a vantage point that allows me to treat them as adults. After they warm up, I call them all to the mound. I start laying the ground work with an official introduction. "My name is Mel Machuca. You can call me Mel or coach or twenty." My uniform number is twenty and I have a habit of calling players by their number. "Mr. Machuca is my father and he's not your coach, I am! So please don't call me that!" This is my first step to building a peer relationship with them; that alone is different than what they're used to. I tell them how long our practices will be and I never violate that time allocation.

In addition, I tell them the importance of attendance. I do this in a way to make it unmistakable, memorable but not authoritarian. "There are only two reasons for missing a practice or a game. A death in the family, your own, or getting lucky in the afternoon! The second one is there because at your age there are things more important than baseball!" I get a surprised look and then a chuckle of disbelief.

"He didn't really say that, did he?" they're thinking.

"Okay let's do it!" Now we begin, in our first practice I have each player take the position he thinks he wants to play. I always do it that way. The players look around, make a mental note and somehow find empty spots on the field or as a last resort they'll ask me where I want them; so far no problems.

The next step is to hit infield practice and it goes more smoothly than I have ever seen it go on the first day. This, in part, is thanks to the returning players. I follow with outfield practice and I can't believe the arms I have in the outfield. At first glance, this is an American Legion coach's dream, three players have already completed a year of college and all but four have completed their senior year of high school. I have a superior infield and eight pitchers.

Right after we finish outfield practice, I call the team into the dugout, look at them and say, "You're the best team I've ever seen; nobody in the state can beat you. We're going to win the State Championship." They look at me as though they have heard that kind of rah-rah before, so they don't let it bother them and may not even buy it. However, I am serious when I say it. Incidentally, this is the first team that ever heard me say that.

I then let them have batting practice. I don't like batting practice. It takes too long and is boring. To hurry things up, I set up two pitchers side by side to alternate throwing. My emphasis is always on defense. I know that more games are lost by mistakes than are won by hitting. These guys have a head start in this department because they are so sound in fielding fundamentals.

Another step is to get them to lose their fear of making mistakes. Being afraid to make a mistake often makes players too rigid and becomes the cause of more mistakes and takes all the fun out of the game. In the majors line scores include runs, hits and errors. It's also why you have a backup man behind the man who's covering the bag on throws.

I let them know that I analyze each and every game but my purpose isn't to place blame. I analyze them to define clearly where we are and what we need to work on. I believe that a baseball season is a continuum and if you work at it you will get better as you go. Getting them to buy into what we have to do to improve is the tougher part. I try to do this routinely in one-on-one conversations walking on the field from position-to- position in practice.

Some of the players assess the talent we have and think that some of our players never make an error. They're convinced that they have to reach that level to be on this team.

What needs to follow is to show them that we are playing at a higher level. I tell them to wear long pants or baseball pants and long sleeve shirts to practice. I tell them to clean and polish their spikes and take care of all of their equipment; the Clay players are already doing this. I tell them to wear cups at all times on the field. These are minor things but needed for higher level differentiation purposes as well as safety. I give them sized hats, as opposed to adjustable ones; for many of them it is the first time that they have ever had them. We have two full sets of uniforms, whites for home games and grays for the road. In addition we have a navy blue Jersey that will match both the white and the gray pants so that we can change when we're playing double headers. Most of the players already believe that this is a step up.

As to practice intensity versus game intensity, they are the same. I reinforce the idea that you play like you practice. So in our practices we run everywhere, run everything out and always throw hard. In infield practice we always go by the numbers; catch the ball then turn, set our feet and step into the throw. There are no glove flips or sideway tosses. We practice what we do in games with ground balls, fly balls and running the bases. When we have batting practice, ground balls are always double plays and balls going to the outfield are throws to third. I don't believe in trick plays; the "This week in baseball" plays happen on TV because of situations that arise and are completed only because the players are fundamentally strong.

At the beginning of the year our team, like most years, is a bell curve in almost every category. To name a few; game experience ranges from one player with seventy –two college games to a few who didn't play in high school in 1977. Those who played a high school season have thirty games under their belts by the time they get here. Our skill level also mirrors that bell curve. We have what we need but in three levels of skill; elite players, strong players and role players but make no mistake everyone has strong fundamental skills. Our tournament experience is just as diverse. Some are high school sectional and regional winners, our returning players won the American Legion Sectional Tournament the previous year.

My next goal is to begin building them into a single unit. For this to happen some of them have to be moved into new positions. Knowing that they come from different high school programs helps to facilitate this. They know the abilities of their high school teammates but not those of the players from the other schools. After seeing the talent, it's apparent that they are sticking around mainly to see what might develop.

One real worry is that we have only one tested catcher and he has bad knees. We need him to stay healthy through double headers during the regular season and in tournaments. Because of this, my job is to multitask. I have to start our season and search for a second catcher. I start asking around and actually tried several young men but can't find what we need. The season is looming and I'm still not ready. We had a very good season last year and I believe that with those returning who are now a year older and stronger we'll be even better.

Greg Heyde has entered the picture by virtue of having played with Post 308 in 1976. When that post decided not to field a team in 1977, Greg virtually became a free agent with very specific limitations. Those limitations are defined by American Legion rules which state that he can complete his eligibility with another American Legion team so long as that team does not exceed the total enrollment rule. Additionally, if more than one team can and is willing to accept him he will have to play for the team nearest his legal residence. Unfortunately, Post 357 is ½ mile closer to Greg's house than Post 50 is.

In order for me to get him, I will have to negotiate with the dark side; Paul Eitler and Joe Derda are the coaches of Post 357, our arch rival. They know who Greg is and want him, and even if they don't, the fact that I do, will negate the possibility of their releasing him outright. I try to meet with them at their post, again as they are scouting high school players, and now at a few of their early practices. After about ten or twelve tries, I finally corner Paul Eitler at a game in Warsaw. I say to him that I gave Greg a choice and that his response was that if he doesn't play for Post 50 he won't play American Legion Baseball at all. Paul's heart, although he won't admit it, is in the right place and he signs the release on the spot.

We now have fifteen on the roster but I still have to find a second catcher who can play at this level. We need to find a way to pull them together as a team. I know it takes time and in order to move forward I'll have to establish a definitive difference between my program and where they came from as a starting point. I have to start building relationships with them and have them begin building relationships with their teammates.

It all begins with trust. Trust changes people; they become what you tell them you expect. I need my players to trust me or I'm not going to get through to them. This is easier said than done. Many of the differences between players have to do with the relationships they had with their high school coaches. Some things have to be undone while others have to be continued. Mutual respect must be part of it. The one thing we have in common is a love of the game.

What I, as a coach, need to see initially is if the game is too fast for them. The biggest difference in any sport as you advance up the levels is the speed with which the game is played. As they mature, players get stronger, run faster, throw and hit harder. If one can anticipate the plays and think as fast as the game is moving, he won't be overwhelmed. This portion of the season begins with the two-day tryouts and moves into the seven preseason practice sessions. I need to see the team practice, not play. Simply stated, players get more chances with the ball in practices than they do in games.

My initial move to start the season is to establish a preliminary pitching rotation. As a matter of fact our early season confidence centers on the fact that we have eight experienced, tournament tested pitchers. This is my third year in South Bend and I haven't had a lefty yet. Our pitching profile is composed of two heaters, five finesse pitchers and a curve ball pitcher. Very few teams at this level ever have this many pitchers. I feel that this group is strong enough to carry us to the state finals. From what I've seen or heard they're all thinkers and understand ball movement, speed changes and location pitching according to the count on the hitter and his position in the batting order.

My coaching philosophies as to playing time are consistent during any season and throughout my career. In double headers, I will start nine in one game and a different nine in the second game. Furthermore, regardless of how we're doing in a particular game I will finish with the players I start the game with exclusive of necessary pitching changes. When tournament time arrives I go with my best nine. Of this number, seven are position players and two are catchers and I hope that by then, I have a final, established pitching rotation.

This team's skill level will make it difficult to discern those nine because we have so many pitchers who are strong in other positions as well. On most teams, especially at the younger levels, it's a given that the pitchers are the best athletes and usually play other positions. At the high school level, however, players begin to specialize.

Our first three games allow us to compare our talent with some of the regional talent. There are no surprises, but we aren't exactly pressed. In the third game something unexpected happens. Dennis Janiszewski, who is pitching a no hitter through the first three innings, dives headfirst back into first base and jams the first finger of his pitching hand on the bag, breaking it and putting him out for the next six weeks at least. I'm not sure how losing this caliber of pitcher this early in the year is going to impact the team.

Our first loss comes in our fourth game. In Valparaiso we lose the front end of a double header 3-1. In the nightcap we're able to come from behind scoring 4 runs in the top of the seventh and take a 12-11 lead in what is our first slugfest. We think we're home free until we walk the bases full with two out in the bottom of the last inning. Most of our pitchers are spent and we're playing a double header tomorrow, so I decide to bring in our strong armed shortstop, Bill Schell, to pitch. As he's warming up, his father walks to the end of the dugout where I'm standing and looks quizzically at me. I turn to him and ask, "Can he pitch?"

"No not really, but he has one helluva pickoff move to first!" he says as a matter of fact.

Upon completing his warm up pitches, Schell goes into a stretch and promptly whirls around and fires to first picking off the runner and ending the game. We win. Enough said.

In his second trip to the plate against Valparaiso in the nightcap, Dave Hankins, who didn't bat in High School because of the Designated Hitter rule, hits a ground ball just out of the reach of the second baseman that makes it to the edge of the outfield grass. That hit makes him one for June and he is elated. Dave is again superb on the mound in two innings of relief. He rides home with me because his Dad isn't there. On the way home I ask him, "What are you going to tell your father about how you pitched today?" Without hesitation Dave answers, "I'm not going to tell him about my pitching, I'm going to tell him about the hit."

We win the next three games, beating Knox 5-0 and Warsaw in a double header, but we outmatch them since they're only drawing from one high school. These are teams that I placed on our schedule to give them a chance at a better level of competition. I invite and try a couple of people behind the plate in an increasingly frustrating attempt to find a partner for a very solid Scott Madey. I still have John Ross who caught for the Clay Angels, a high school summer team in the younger leagues. He homers against Warsaw but right now I need a catcher. Ross works hard and if push comes to shove he can fill in. I sense, however, that even though he is willing to do it, he's more comfortable in the infield than behind the plate. I know I have to keep searching.

Early in the season the players and coaches are on different wave lengths. Most players think that I am looking for no errors and 1.000 batting averages. I'm not. I'm simply trying to see if the players can cover the defensive positions. The second question I need answered is, can they be part of a team or are they just playing for themselves?

The changes that I need to make are becoming clearer. I want to create a team where we are two deep everywhere but consistently stable. Each player has to have comfort in the knowledge that when he is on the field he will be seeing the field the same way in every game. The playing field looks different when you're in different positions. Just throwing a player into an open spot does not help to strengthen your defensive play.

Since we don't have a career first baseman I move both Jim Andert from second base and Marc Toles from shortstop to first and inform them that I need them to make that their new home. Both are tall and have infielders' hands. They also know that they are in competition for that spot. They have to get comfortable covering that new territory because the move makes the field look different to both of them. I leave Vargyas where he is but move Kowatch from backup second baseman to right field. Our beginning strengths are at shortstop and third base with Shell and Coker so I make a decision to use Will Shepherd as the only utility man for both positions on the left side of the infield. I will also use Will in the outfield because I need his bat in the lineup. This makes our infield solid regardless of who is on the field.

Mike Clarke, a pitcher/center fielder, is a returning college freshman who anchors our outfield extremely well with his speed and maturity. Dave Yates who is a pitcher- third baseman is moved to left field with Greg Heyde; that way we will have strong arms no matter who's in the lineup. Right field is open but I have some time to think about it and have several possibilities including three other pitchers. Arm strength can't be compromised in right field, because that's the longest throw.

None of these decisions is made at a meeting. Each is made on the field, as a result of what we see. We appear to be a work in progress and it seems that except for the pitching, every time we take the field we have people in different positions.

Our last game prior to our midseason trip to southern Indiana is against the Adams High School summer team. They're younger than we are, but need to play us in order for them to see better competition. I use three different catchers in the double header and after it ends, Coach Buczkowski comes over to me and says, "I didn't realize how much talent you really had until I saw your team today, nice game! Your only question mark seems to be behind the plate."

I responded with, "Yes, I know. I've tried a lot of kids back there but can't seem to find one who can hold our pitchers. Guess I'll have to keep looking. You wouldn't consider giving me Romeo would you?" I ask not wanting to sound like I'm begging. His answer is a God send.

"I'll give you Romeo if you'll take another one of my players with him. I couldn't possibly allow only one to play on your team. It would seem like total favoritism. Besides that, I still have my season to consider." He states firmly.

"Who else do you want me to take?" I ask. "We're pretty strong everywhere else."

His unhesitating reply is "A center fielder, named Dan Szajko."

I agree immediately in order to get Romeo. I don't know Szajko, but I do know that coach Butch wouldn't give me anyone he didn't think was ready.

So they're added with the stipulation that they have to play in their high school games if there is a conflict of schedule. We now have a full roster and we're at least two deep at every position even though they won't join us until the 4th of July Tournament.

We start our season searching for the combination that will be the most competitive. We win nine out of the first ten games but we're still tentative and playing as individuals. By design, this is the weakest part of our schedule and we still aren't blowing teams away even though we're winning. Our first real test will come on a trip to Indianapolis this weekend, where we will play two strong teams who perennially get pretty far in the tournament It will also give me a chance to see how this group can perform away from home on and off the field and help our players start building relationships with each other. An important step is to room them by position not by the schools they come from.

BOTTOM OF THE 2^(ND)

Our tryouts and first practices of the year gave us a glimpse of what we had. I remember them being crisp, and I came away being impressed with our possibilities in all phases of the game, but especially our defense. We had players who could cover ground and had very good hands, instincts, and arms. That's a recipe for good defense. Offensively, I knew I could contribute to this team from the beginning. I was coming off a very good senior season and even though I initially might have thought I could compete with everyone in the power department, my strength was making solid contact and not striking out. I hadn't seen the Adams guys play in person so when I first saw Jeff Coker swing a bat I was like everyone else who thought to themselves..."Oh my God"! His bat speed was the best I had ever seen and he didn't just hit the ball, he crushed it. As I looked around it seemed to me to be a very balanced lineup, with good athletes in every spot.

I was very anxious and looking forward to the start of our season. Jeff Kowatch and I had never experienced a sectional championship in high school. We had been Conference Champions but the end of the year championships eluded us all three years, so for us this was a chance to experience big time winning, possibly on a grand scale. We had been .500 in all three high school seasons and we just figured with this kind of pitching depth and athleticism at every position, how could we not win a ton?

Our schedule in the beginning of the year was mediocre to good. We played a few really competitive teams, but mostly we had our opponents at a disadvantage. Mel was very busy trying to put the pieces of the puzzle together, at a number of positions defensively, and our batting lineup. I was moved to the outfield for the first time in my baseball career. Toles and "Dert" (Andert) were moved to first base. Kowatch joined me in the outfield for the first time in his career also. All four of us were versatile enough to play both infield and outfield positions so it gave Mel many options. Catching was a concern for a variety of reasons. The guys who did catch early in the season had a wide variety of experience, and they were catching guys who could really pitch and could get it up to the plate with something on it.

Our only loss in this first stretch of games was when I took a loss on the mound at Valparaiso in a double-header. I remember thinking after the game that I hadn't pitched terribly, but the bottom line was they defeated us 3-1 for our first loss. How they held our lineup to only one run is hard to imagine, but they did. I remember many different lineups in the beginning of our season, but a few guys had spots in our batting order locked up and that was okay, because every team needs a few definites, and we had them.

I believe many of us were pressing a bit in the beginning trying to earn time and our spots. And it wasn't so much to impress the coach as it was our teammates. We wanted to prove we belonged. Our coach and our teammates needed to know they could count on us to make plays. Maybe that's why in the long run it took us a while to jell completely as a unit. We started off our season well though; going 9-1 in our first ten games.

Injuries hurt our pitching staff early in the season. But the flip side of that is it gave some opportunities for other guys to step up and earn some innings on the mound. Jano suffered a broken a finger diving back into first base in his first start for us. I had been really looking forward to watching him do his thing. Clarke had a bad pitching shoulder and that was our second major starter who would be shelved. In my mind's eye as I looked at our pitching staff early on, I could see "Hank"(Hankins), Heyde, Jano, and Clarke getting most of the innings, with maybe three or four of us getting relief duty or mop up innings. A quality pitching staff to be sure, but the injuries forced Mel to add depth to our pitching staff in ways that he probably hadn't envisioned at the start of the year.

In the end, I think the injuries forced us to become a better team, a closer unit if you will. I'm not sure exactly how much the playing time would have been different had the injuries not occurred, but it certainly got more guys involved and that was a good thing. Ownership...a team must possess that feeling to reach its full potential. I'm a firm believer in that concept, and learned it at the ripe old age of 18. Unselfishness...for some individuals and teams it might be a problem, they might not be mature enough, but this team never seemed to struggle with it outwardly. For that I am truly grateful. Even early on in this summer season, I think we all had a pretty good sense of team. Mel was a great role model for that attitude. He was up front with his thoughts about playing time and he never gave anyone a feeling of getting messed over, mainly because he always did what he said he would do...accountability. Responsibility... He had his and we had ours. A solid working relationship. But there is a fine line between how selfish and focused you had to be to make plays and show you could be counted on, and playing and supporting your teammates for the team to do well.

To see the field on a consistent basis for this team you had to put up some numbers and make some plays on defense. Were people disappointed they weren't playing every inning of every game? Yes, we were a team full of good, competitive players, but there are only nine spots in every game, and we had a lot more than nine good players. Someone would always have to be waiting for their opportunity. How do you handle that as a player, or as a coach? With class is our standard answer. Some of us learned that at different stages of that summer. It was important that Mel give all the players some chances and for everyone to become involved as teammates. What really helped all of us, especially Mel, is the fact that we were all good athletes and could adjust well to playing different positions.

At this early stage of the season what really pleased me was the fun I was having with everyone. We seemed to mesh pretty well from the beginning. Obviously, it took a while for everyone to feel totally comfortable with each other, but it was clear from the beginning that this would be a really great group, especially for the jacking around stuff that always happens on teams.

We lost at least one player who decided this wasn't for him. That's not surprising really because this type of schedule was a real commitment of time and energy. Not to mention the talent level. It's not for everyone, it isn't CYO baseball anymore at this level. Schell was used to it playing in Texas for his university, and the guys returning knew our coach was continually trying to upgrade the schedule, and we had played around 40 games the summer before, so we knew what to expect. Mel was serious and so were we.

Humor was a big part of this team. Some teams try too hard to make each other laugh and tease each other to the point of becoming obnoxious. With us, it was baseball first, then the BS. Sometimes it happens during games or practices, but we had a very good work ethic, and winning was important to us. You could sense that from the very beginning. It was just the right amount of messing around. We stayed loose but were poised to compete at a high level. And what made it especially great for me were the different types of personalities and slants on humor that this group had. Such diversity, more than I had experienced with any other team up to that point in my life. Most of the guys genuinely made me laugh. And that's a good combo for a summer day when you're 18 years old, and you know your world is going to get at least a little more serious in about three months, and you're not quite sure you're ready for that. Very high level baseball and jacking around, just what the doctor ordered.

The key is the ability to turn it on and off. For the vast majority of our team it was not a problem. When it was time to make plays we were in the moment. We knew where and when we could afford to cut up a little, and that's a fine line with teams of athletes. You go too far and it's the Jackie Gleason Comedy Hour instead of championship level baseball. Not far enough and baseball can sometimes seem like the Bataan Death March. Our team was right smack dab in the middle, knowing and sensing the moments that deserved to be laughed at. It never felt strained with this team for me. Comfort levels were reached that made the baseball stuff that much more enjoyable. The coaching staff set a great tone from the beginning with this team. It just got better and better.

＂＂

Jeff Coker # 19
I remember walking from the dugout to my car at Clay Park after a tough sectional loss to Clay High School (3-2), when a man approached me about playing for American Legion Post 50 that summer. I don't recall my exact answer, but I believe it was something mundane like…Okay.

Tryouts that summer were at Bellville and Boland Parks. Two recollections at these tryouts were, "What fielding position did Mel Machuca have in mind for me", and secondly, after facing Greg Heyde in an intra-squad game, "where does a guy that size (5'8", 160 lbs.) come up with such an overpowering explosive fastball"? I recall saying to myself, "he may be a 'tad' bit difficult for opposing teams' hitters".

Andert #7
I had just spent 4 years competing against these yahoos and now I was supposed to be a teammate? Scared?? Absolutely ….These were guys who were really, really good. Natural athletes to whom the game came easily. I don't recall hitting anything out of the infield during that tryout, When Mel told us when the first game was and I was in, I didn't really know how or why, but I was in and I was ready to go!

Madey #12
The first day of tryouts was a little disconcerting, it was immediately

clear these guys were good and if I made the team it would be the best collection of talent I had ever played with. The odd thing was that it wasn't a cutthroat atmosphere; friendships immediately started forming, even amongst folks going for the same positions. Mel's ability to create a relaxed atmosphere where you just went out and played was evident from the first day I met him and it is my opinion probably the most important attribute that made us a team.

VARGYAS #15
Even early on we were a group of guys who seemed to know how to play together. We really didn't struggle or fight about playing time, for some reason that wasn't a concern. It was about how much we enjoyed playing the game and hanging around with one another.

RUDASICS #8
I remember pitching at Warsaw down there and throwing a five or six-inning one hitter. We won by ten runs or more.

HEYDE #2
Mel always made sure I had what I needed. He bought my cleats for me, made sure I shined them and always made sure I didn't look like a Podunk hillbilly from Mishawaka. Believe it or not you really do play better when you look like a ball player.

3RD INNING

The Nadir & Resurgence

"Boiling Point"

TOP OF THE 3RD

East Chicago, Indiana in Northwest Indiana, where I grew up, is really an extension of Chicago. There is a narrow stretch of land about eighty miles wide extending east from the Illinois state line to South Bend, IN. that is definitively part of the northern United States. The width of that strip is bordered on the north by Lake Michigan and on the south by US 6 which seems to be an extension of the Mason-Dixon Line, if you will, which is, to the best of my recollection, where the Deep South begins.

In high school in the northern part of the state if you have a good team and you win the local tournaments, you then go "down state" to play for state recognition. I can't begin to describe for you what that means other than you are taking urban people completely out their element and throwing them into a quagmire. In the years prior and through the 1970's only basketball teams were subjected to this because of a one-class tournament system which resulted in a single state champion and was nationally recognized as "Hoosier Hysteria".

Likewise in American Legion Baseball, advancing in the state tournament takes you toward Southern Indiana which is a hotbed of baseball as well as basketball. Knowing that, I always schedule a weekend overnight baseball trip to see what the competitive levels of the teams are and to give our team a chance to have an overnight away from home and get to know each other a little better and perhaps do some relationship building.

Our early season success occurred with very little serious effort but what happens next brings us back to reality. There is a lack of focus, a lack of intensity. A lot of people are waiting for their teammate to step up and make something happen or at least take the lead. I have the feeling that people are not ready to accept responsibility for what is happening. Romeo and Szajko have not yet joined us because they have a weekend commitment with their high school team.

It's on this trip that we first hear the comparatives, "bigger and stronger". We split a double header with Southport where we escape within an inch of our lives. This year's Southport team is big and strong and has good pitching. It is the type of team we will be meeting later in the year so splitting with them isn't even close to what we need to be doing. Dave Hankins loses the first game (his first loss of the season) and Dave Yates wins the night cap.

The next day we travel to Beech Grove, a team with players that look like "Big John" they "stand six feet six and weigh 245" or so it seems that day. To top it off they have a huge field with a pasture where center field should be. The sign reads 410 feet from home plate but I think it is more like the proverbial country mile. In the opener they beat us 6-3 and in the second game we score 8 runs but they rally and score nine to sweep the double header. It's apparent that four back-to-back double headers, albeit not on consecutive days, is about two too many for our pitching staff. Even with our experienced pitchers we don't have enough to get it done. I was even forced to pitch Jeff Coker who hasn't pitched since Little League. The only highlight on this trip is a tape measure shot by Jeff that he hits well over the 410 mark in center field. Although it brings a lot of ooh's and ah's it doesn't bring us a win. They literally run us out of town on a rail. Thank goodness we're on our way home to our own Holiday Tournament.

What I saw on this trip is a team of talented players who are not playing fundamentally sound baseball. The team that I think is making such great strides toward becoming a championship unit seems to have taken a giant step backward. Losing to those teams in Indianapolis the way we did is definitely a signal. In those three losses we gave up 18 runs and if you add our winning game our opponents totaled 26 runs in only four games. Giving up over six runs a game to these teams is totally unacceptable. This happens even in view of the fact that we have seven starting pitchers even with Janiszewski still out.

Clearly, I have to change something in my approach to coaching this group. I have to get back to working on our fundamentals and at the same time get the point across to them that this is their team, not mine and that this is their season, not mine. I have to sit down and reevaluate everything I have done so far. I think that what bothers me the most is that I seem to be the only one on the team that truly feels these losses.

The opening game of our Holiday Tournament is an extension of the weekend. Even the term lackluster insufficiently describes what happens to us in that 4-0 loss to Michigan City. I have to move fast and I sit everybody down in the dugout to get a dialogue going. Nobody wants to speak. I can feel their frustration, loss of direction and total lack of focus. This is my chance to get them thinking about how they are playing but I lose my temper when I can't get through to them. In my frustration I finally say "Look, I'm going to win the state championship this year with you or without you! If you want to come along with me, be here for practice tomorrow to start working seriously on our game. If you don't want to come with me, don't let the gate hit you in the ass as you leave."

Just then I hear a loud crack and I turn just in time to see that Jeff Coker has shattered my fungo bat, slamming it on the fence pole next to the dugout wall. I verbally jump on him immediately and demand in no uncertain tone, "Why'd you do that?"

His response demonstrates his total frustration as to what is happening with the team. It's hard for him because he knows he's going to be signed at the end of the summer by a major league team. This program is only giving him a place to play until that happens. He snaps back with, "This is bull shit! I'm going home!"

Because of what happened with the team this weekend and because he had to sit on the bench for the first time in his life in some of those games, nothing is making any sense to him. Jeff can't see the course I'm taking to bring this team together and certainly can't see where we're going.

Even knowing that, I can't let this incident pass or I will lose control of the group, I have to take decisive action now. I say without hesitation, "Okay; Go! You're off the team; anyone want to go with him?" Silence follows. Everyone is stunned, but no one else leaves. I have just kicked northern Indiana's strongest high school player and our team's game-breaker off the team in front of everyone. The All State third baseman who had put on a hitting display at the North-South High School All Star Game is gone. This move makes an undeniable statement about my beliefs as to the importance of the team over any individual player. I have just snatched back all the empowerment I had given them in one single move. They immediately know that I am totally serious about how this program has to run. Now each man has to decide how we're going to be able to move forward together as a team. This is a difficult challenge for them and me. I, as their coach, have to find a way to bring them back together and trust that I have taken the right action.

It's important to understand that elite players are like thoroughbred race horses. Everything about them is extreme. This includes their talent as well as their passion and emotions. They need only to be able to see the entire track ahead of them and know exactly where the finish line is; anything going on around them is a distraction. When distractions occur, they become extremely disoriented and agitated. The greatest race horses have trainers who are able to assess situations and get the horses back on track to control and direct their energy in order to perform at their peak level every time they get into the starting gate.

I am beginning to understand that Jeff's biggest problem isn't with the team, it's that he can't merge his personal goals with our team's goals. Jeff was arguably the premier hitter in all of Indiana this past high school season. He is a one swing game breaker. He doesn't hit the long ball. The ball literally explodes off of his bat. One of the longest home runs I have ever seen hit by an amateur or a professional was hit by Jeff Coker. It was in an Adams High School Baseball game when he hit a ball over the left field fence over two tennis courts onto the roof of the school.

He is definitely one of our elite players; no one doubts that. No matter what kind of a season he has, he is going to be signed! He is fundamentally strong, very athletic with great physical strength and really knows baseball. It's his life. He had been coached by his father in one of the most successful Little League programs in Indiana and then by Lenny Buczkowski, one of the most successful coaches in Indiana High School Baseball.

Jeff exudes confidence in the field and at the plate. One of the few players I have who uses a wooden bat. He really understands pitching, timing and has tremendous bat speed. Impatience is his weakness, especially when he senses that the people he is playing with or against aren't capable of playing at his level.

Jeff Coker's development on this team is happening at a different pace than the rest of the team but his change is psychological, not in his skill or confidence level. It has more to do with accepting his role as a team leader and being responsible for what happens on the field, regardless of how well he personally plays that day.

I go home that night wondering if I have made the crucial mistake of the season. I speak to my wife about what had happened with Jeff. "I kicked Coker off the team today," I said flatly, waiting to hear her initial reaction. I got her attention.

"Why; what happened?" she asks as she turns toward me. For some reason Lynda sees Jeff differently than I do. I see the ballplayer, she sees the young man. "Talk to him! He needs you and you need him", she states firmly.

Right now, at this moment I can't, I am too angry, and I can't let any player no matter who they are run the team. Forget about losing the games this weekend, they're unimportant compared to losing a player. This truly is the low point of our young season. Games can never be more important than the people playing them!

The necessary changes initially begin as a result of our Indianapolis trip and 4th of July Tournament loss to Michigan City. That horribly played game becomes the initial rallying point for our team. That loss puts us at 10 wins and 5 losses. The only thing I can think of is that this team has completely lost its focus. If this were a business venture we would stop everything, have an emergency meeting and begin to analyze what was happening and why. In baseball that's a little tougher to do because your roster is set and your schedule is set and running.

The rational approach with a baseball team is to ask, what are we doing wrong? You start by doing a personal inventory as objectively as you can. Am I doing all that I can as coach? Do I have the right people? Do I know what their goals are and how they compare with our team goals? Am I using them correctly? Am I calling the right plays? Are we making mistakes on offense, defense or in pitching? Most importantly, are the players and coaches on the same page? Finally, do they believe in me and I in them? We didn't have time to ponder for too long. We had another game in two days but this time without Jeff.

We play and win our next two games without him but it's clear that we have lost something. Coker calls me and requests a second chance, but before I can give it to him I know I have to check with the team. I have been telling them all along it is their team so they have to be a part of this decision, a big part. To accomplish this I elect to let the team vote on it. This is a vehicle I can use to return the initial control of the team I had given them and then suddenly took away in the dugout with the 4th of July incident.

At the end of the second game without Jeff, I hand out small sheets of paper to make it a secret ballot. The mood of the team makes it clear that they are taking this very seriously. They understand that with their vote they are again accepting ownership of the team regardless of the outcome. The silence is deafening as I count the votes, they anxiously wait for the result.

The team's decision is to reinstate Jeff. He has already apologized to me in a one- on-one meeting, now he has to apologize to the team, and sit out a game on the bench in uniform. He does that and from that point on it is a closed issue. It seems as though a weight is lifted off of everyone's shoulders. Our team is back together.

We had won all three of the games he missed but it wasn't the same as when he played. After winning the next three with him back I can't help but think that we are slowly beginning to reach our necessary performance level. Our emergence, however, comes to a screeching halt in a poorly played game and an unexpected loss to Elkhart Post 74. That game increases our losses to 6 against only 16 wins. That Elkhart loss cries out for a total change in our attitudes. Everyone realizes that we need something to change our intensity. That something manifests itself in the form of a team meeting which in turn becomes the kick off point that, if successful, would initiate our evolution. We have to change because our window of opportunity is beginning to shrink and everyone on the team can see it happening. Our eyes appear to be scanning the ground searching for an answer. They are all reluctant to speak at first, but then they start talking.

Jeff Kowatch opens the commentary with a statement. "I don't know about the rest of you, but this is the best team that I have ever played on." "I can't believe the talent that's here and just so you all know, I'm really glad to be whatever part of it I can be." He goes on, "I do know that we're not playing up to our potential and believe me starting today, I 'm going to give it everything I've got and hope that the rest of the team will do the same thing."

This low point in the season again reminds me that managing a baseball team isn't about baseball, it's about people. Jeff Kowatch's heartfelt statement is just what we need to get the team thinking about our potential again and what we set out to accomplish. Others echo similar sentiments.

During this stretch of events our players not only accept the team concept but also come to realize that they are accountable for what happens on the field in each and every game. We only have seven games left on the schedule before the sectional and we still aren't the team we're capable of becoming. One thing is very apparent, we not only have to talk about it, but we have to want it and we have to start working on it now.

BOTTOM OF THE 3ᴿᴰ

INDIANAPOLIS TRIP – DEFINING MOMENT #1

Something that I and our team had been looking forward to turned into something we'd rather forget. I'm pretty sure my teammates feel the same way about it. We had played a marginally competitive schedule up to this point in the season, and enjoyed a lot of success in terms of wins, but this would be a real measuring stick for us. A challenge that needed to be met. We had played pretty good baseball and were looking forward to showcasing our stuff in the Big Town, while Mel was busy giving everyone chances to rise to the top at different positions. We had a few for-sures and everyone knew it and accepted it. Schell was our shortstop. Coker was our third baseman. Our pitching staff had four for-sures but one of them (Jano) was hurt and on the shelf for the foreseeable future with a broken finger, and another solid pitcher who we were counting on to be a go to guy was having problems with his shoulder (Mike Clarke). Heyde and Hank were rocks, always taking their turns and giving us a chance to win. Yates and Rudy were next and trying to stabilize their position in our rotation.

It seemed as though we were playing in a funk all weekend in Indy, but we didn't know why. We ran out of pitching during this trip and Mel had to use everyone. We had many pitchers and on most teams some of us would do quite nicely, but against this level of competition we needed guys who could keep teams' offenses under control, and we lost control in most of our games here, and at the most critical times it seemed. Southport and Beech Grove had good quality teams and players. If you made mistakes with pitches they could and would hurt you. Our defense wasn't tight and right yet either. Sluggish is the word that comes to mind in describing our play in Indy that weekend. We looked and played like a team that was not truly confident in our collective games.

What we didn't see or understand yet is the genius in our coach for scheduling this trip. It did at least three things for us that were instrumental in our tournament success that would come later in late summer. First, it proved to us that we weren't infallible. We were NOT God's gift to the game of baseball. If we played poorly or were not mentally ready to compete at our highest level in every game, there were good teams out there that could beat us. Your basic good dose of humble pie.

Second, it gave us a chance to be together off the field in conditions where we had to get to know each other and live together in a hotel, as individuals with habits and mannerisms that we all had to get used to. The off the field stuff matters. For some teams it makes or breaks them. The cliques and groups must not divide the team emotionally. Mel seemed to keep an eye on that kind of stuff and it would prove crucial for us later in the tournament. Up until this trip we just drove to the games, showed up, and did our thing. This particular weekend trip we were forced to be closer as teammates and roommates.

Third, it was our first real grind. Playing this many games on back-to-back days, in this particular case, double headers, in hot, tough conditions. The toughness of a team, mental and physical, needs to be challenged if a team is ever going to rise to the top, in any sport. We obviously didn't handle that challenge the first time out of the gate. We would have to work on it. It would eventually become a centerpiece to our game, but not at this juncture of our season.

Looking back, it was probably the start of our metamorphosis as a unit of competitors. Forget the talent aspect for a moment. We all found out that weekend a little bit about how each of us felt about losing baseball games and not playing up to our abilities. I was beginning to see that my teammates had the same competitive instinct that I had. We didn't know exactly how to fix what was wrong, but at least I could feel that inside each of us, we were bothered by losses, of any kind. For some young players and teams it can turn into a whining or excuses session of epic proportion. But for our team it did not. Our maturity level was beyond that, but we could not overcome the frustration at that point. For something that was so negative from a win/loss perspective, it turned out in the end to be somewhat of a galvanizing segment of our season.

We obviously had some things that needed fixing. We needed to find a third and fourth starter we could count on, both physically and mentally. We also needed to set the bar much higher for our own individual and team's expectation level in terms of our overall play, in all aspects of the game. In other words, we all could feel that we needed to push our play to the next level. And we needed to realize that we had to play solid in all phases so that teams had to BEAT us, not us beating ourselves with sloppy play or unmotivated periods during games.

It also for some of us became our first major step in traveling for baseball. Some of the team had done some as high school players on spring trips, and for Schell this was old news as a college player already. Clarke and Vargyas had been away at college also. But for many of us, it was that first step in being away from what is comfortable, and convenient. Northern Indiana we knew. Indianapolis and all that it entails is another story. Our confidence was not quite where we needed it to be and it showed in our play.

For those teams that defeated us that weekend, I have often wondered if they even knew we won the National Championship later that summer, and went undefeated in the tournament. For those that did they must have wondered how in the world did THAT team accomplish such a daunting task? We certainly didn't look or play like a champion, that's for sure. I'd like to call us a work still in progress at that point of our season.

When you lose three out of four games there are of course some things you'd like to change. But that's what is great about baseball. You have to live in the here and now. There are so many games that you can't pout about the last one because if you do, the next one will eat you up too. It's called competitive maturity, and we were developing ours in Indianapolis. It was ugly and painful, and not a lot of fun, but I believe so very important in our team's overall maturation process.

We can't change the outcomes of those games in Indianapolis. Nor should we. We didn't play well enough to earn those as wins. The best team that day won those games. It wasn't that we played lousy baseball, just uninspired baseball. What we had to learn was that we couldn't just show up and win. We had to grind it out, like most other athletic teams. Be in each game, emotionally, mentally, and physically. We had to play with heart and guts, and we did not do that during this weekend road trip.

I can't speak for my coach, but I believe he learned a lot about us that weekend. Some of our weaknesses were exposed. Some areas of growth were identified. That my friends, is why he scheduled it in the first place - to put his team under some fire in a more hostile environment. He knew we needed to be put into some unfamiliar situations, to see who would respond, and who would not. To get a feel also for the rest of the state and the level of competition we hoped to face later in our season.

Testing the troops. Every leader needs to do it, to find out what they've really got to work with. We didn't respond very well to the challenge as a team, but we all came out of it with a realistic view of ourselves, and for most of us we didn't like what we saw.

We grew from it, but it is the kind of growth that you don't recognize initially as a player. It's always there, somewhere inside you, when you don't play well, but does it affect your play in the future? Does it cause you to make changes in your approach to the competition and your game? Does it or can it have positive benefits when you fail and look bad doing it? For us of course the answer is yes. Maybe not right away, as we still had some growing and maturing to do as a team. But the experience we gained both on and off the field that weekend would prove to be valuable. I guess you could say it was a lose-win situation. It's just that the benefits we had to wait on a little while longer.

It definitely was a defining moment in our season though. That we cannot deny. Some questions were answered. For some of us, we came away with the feeling that we, and possibly our coach, no longer considered ourselves viable options as pitchers on this team. And that was O.K. We and our coach needed to know that anyway. I believe my amateur pitching career ended that day in Beech Grove (as it should have) and I'm no worse for the wear. My last game as a pitcher was a nightmare. It was short and not so sweet. I was supposed to put out the flames. The scoreboard lit up like a Christmas tree on fire. I didn't have the stuff needed to do the job. We tried to stay in the game by finally waking up our offense but it wasn't' enough. We lost the slugfest and I took the loss as the pitcher of record. Thank you very much. I and some of my teammates would have to contribute to this team in other ways, at other positions, and on offense.

HOLIDAY TOURNAMENT– DEFINING MOMENT #2

The real low point of our regular season was reached in our Fourth of July Holiday Tournament. We had just returned from our debacle of a road trip to Indianapolis with more questions than answers as to where this team was heading. We lost to a very average Michigan City team 4-0. It was bad. Real bad. No juice. Going through the motions, everyone kind of playing for themselves. We were exhausted, physically and mentally. A disconnected team is the best way to describe us during and after that game at Rockne Field near St. Joe High School.

Mel had finally seen enough of that kind of play from us. He gathered us together in the dugout and let us know that it was totally unacceptable. He challenged all of us to really ask ourselves if playing the way were capable of and winning the state championship was worthy of our effort and time. He told us NOT to come back to practice on Monday if we weren't ready to commit to that, and if not, find something else to do for the summer.

Right as he was finishing his come to Jesus sermon, we all hear this sound. Baseball players know it instinctually. It's unmistakable. It's the sound of a bat hitting something very hard. When we all locate where the noise was coming from, we realize that our power hitting third baseman, Jeff Coker, had just busted Mel's fungo bat into pieces on a corner of the dugout by the foul ball fence...oops! We were all just waiting for the ax to fall, the fireworks to start, the fight to begin, or whatever, but this much we knew: Mel was going to have to deal with this, and deal with it right now. He did.

He asked Jeff why he did that, which looking back now, was a perfectly good question to ask him. I wanted to know also. Probably my teammates as well. You'll have to ask them. I don't remember exactly what Jeff said. I can't quote him, but I do remember feeling that it was just an immature act by a frustrated member of a struggling team. At that point, Mel says to him that he's done with this team, and anyone else who wants to join him in the parking lot please feel free to go. You could have heard a pin drop. One of the best players in the state of Indiana, the star of the North-South High School All-Star Series, and more importantly to us a key part of our offense had just been kicked off by far the best team I had ever been a part of.

At the time I remember thinking that this was BIG. I didn't pretend to know exactly how it would affect everyone, but you can't lose a player of Jeff's ability without having to make some key changes. Would we respond? Was Coker really going to walk away from this team? We knew Mel was serious. Did we have enough to make up for his absence? No one else got up to leave. For me, that was critical. I knew the guys who stayed in that dugout, and I believed we all would, were going to respond to the challenge from our coach. I just wanted the chance to play again, to get the bad taste out of my mouth about how we had played during this stretch. With or without Jeff, I just wanted our team to play again and play well.

We had too many very good baseball players not to be a force in the state tournament. I wanted badly to be on a championship team, but to that point had not developed the leadership skills necessary to be one of our key leaders on the field. A good piece to the puzzle I guess, but not the one to carry the sword into battle. I never saw myself in that role on this team anyway, even though I had the most experience at Post 50.

From the splintered pieces of that fungo bat, a team would emerge eventually that I have trouble describing to people. From the ashes as they say. There was nowhere to go but up. We had felt the lowest of lows when Jeff walked away that day, all the while all of us trying to digest the last half a dozen games which had been nightmarish. I don't know how long it was but before too much time had passed Jeff had talked to Mel and apologized for his explosion, and apologized to us as a team for it also. I can't remember the timing of it all. But the bottom line was that within a few days or a week, we had our third baseman back and we would start the uphill climb to where we wanted to be.

At this point we were not near where everyone knew we should be as a unit. We were like a really powerful race car engine that was missing for some reason, sputtering and misfiring for no apparent justifiable reason. We couldn't put our finger on it, and I don't think Mel had all the answers yet either, but we sure were struggling to find ourselves.

Up to this point in our season we had been playing selfishly, individually. Mel wanted us to fight as a unit, a team. We were not there yet. We had been so busy trying to perfect our own games and earn playing time that we had our eyes no where near the prize. We were talented individuals but not a strong unit per se. We needed something to bring us together, so we could appreciate each other's talents and focus on winning games as a group rather than how much success am I having today. Selfishness, it wasn't at the level where others could easily see it with our team, it was much more covert in nature, but present none the less. What that "thing" was that we needed was nowhere in sight, but we needed it NOW or we were going to be remembered as the most under-achieving talented team in the history of our area. It was coming though...and just in time.

ELKHART LOSS – TEAM MEETING – DEFINING MOMENT #3

We started to play better after the Holiday Tournament loss. How many wins until the Elkhart game I can't exactly remember but we were at least starting to make better efforts. Then we play Elkhart, a team that some of us had history with as high school rivals. From our low point against Michigan City we had built up a little momentum. Some things were starting to come together for us a little.

Our attitudes and approach were better, not great mind you. We had a ways to go yet, but better. We were at least competing in games with more enthusiasm and juice. We didn't seem to be as fragmented, or cliquish. By this point in our season, relation-ships were beginning to form between guys that had been playing against each other for many years. We were individuals from four competing high schools that had a few things in common. The new guys were starting to feel more comfortable around the vet-erans and vice versa. We were starting to get to know each other as people, not just teammates. This was an important development. The friendships were beginning to meld together better. We were beginning to appreciate each other in new and different ways.

Then the Elkhart game, which turned out to be our sixth loss of the season. It was extremely competitive because we knew those guys and they knew us. To say there was no love in the house or on the field would be putting it mildly. They had talent, and so did we. They made more plays that day and we had to choke down a very painful defeat. We thought we might be over the hump, then this, to of all teams, Elkhart. The kettle was ready. It was hot enough finally. Boiling point had been reached.

I don't remember who exactly, but someone called a team meeting after that last loss, and some players finally opened up and said what was on their minds. It ran the full gambit, from controlled evaluation, to some very colorful foul language. No one was exempt from the storm. But this much was sure. We were finally out there…emotionally exposed, as competitors within a team. No hidden agendas anymore. For our coach, this is exactly what was needed. No more trying to look like big league phenoms. Looking flashy and cool was out. Playing for stats and yourself was out. Playing tough and nasty was in, and playing for our team to win games was in, and we were all good with that. We were finally at our breaking point as far as losing baseball games.

I honestly can't remember if I said anything at that team meeting in the dugout or not. It didn't really matter though. What was important for me and my teammates was that it was finally all out there on the table. I am not sure to this day if we would have reached the level of play we finally ascended to without this come to Jesus talk after Elkhart. Maybe, maybe not. But all of us could feel a sense of urgency. The tournament was coming up soon and we were way too competitive to let this thing spiral out of control. We were done with it. Emotionally and psychologically we were raising the bar. A turning of the page so to speak. It was a conscious, collective decision made by our entire team. Our first real and best commitment to each other. It's what great teams need to do with and for each other.

KOWATCH #1

I remember after the weekend in Indianapolis that I thought this team was going nowhere. I think it was definitely a low time for the team and probably me. The thing that I learned from that point on was the importance of commitment, perseverance and faithfulness.

ANDERT #7

To me Jeff Coker was the epitome of the natural athlete. He never looked like he was working at the game. Here was a guy who would habitually suck down Sweet Tarts and have the nonchalant attitude of chewing on his fingernails, all the while processing every pitch, every out, and every tendency that the opponent threw at him.

HANKINS #14

The advantages we gained by adding speed and athleticism to our strong fundamentals was lost by our poor execution during this part of our season. Our hearts and our heads just weren't in it.

COKER #19

I will always appreciate Mel and his wife Lynda for treating me like family off the field. As a teenager I had some issues, even though at that time it was a little difficult to understand. They always gave me the impression that they had a genuine fondness for me.

4ᵀᴴ INNING

The Transformation

"The will to win isn't nearly as important as the will to prepare to win."

R. Knight

TOP OF THE 4ᵀᴴ

Our record is sixteen wins against only six losses but we are playing like any other team. After the team meeting, we agree that we are ready to prove that we can achieve our primary goal of winning the state championship. We verbally commit to not lose again. I wonder how many players actually believe that. Each player has to scour his psyche and take a full personal inventory from his skills to his inner ambitions to reexamine how he fits into our team's goals. All of this to prepare himself for the last lap. The state finals aren't that far away and remain within our reach if we can maintain our focus long enough to take advantage of the opportunity. For my part, I decide to reiterate that we need to be successful an inning at a time. The team seems ready to respond. What I need to create here is a culture of winning and now they are finally beginning to see that we are running out of time.

As stated earlier, the substantive change that has to occur with each player is that he has to take ownership of his part of the team. Each component part of the team or each player, as it were, has to be working at maximum efficiency. The big question for the coaching staff is … "How do we get them there." Bill and I talk about it almost daily. We have to get each player to accept this ownership of his position on the field and in the batting order. No longer does he have the luxury of waiting for the elite player to make the big play. If the ball comes into his assigned area he has to make the play himself. If we need him to make something happen on offense he has to do it. That's the beauty of baseball, each player has to do it for himself. He can't hide. Focus becomes the dominant demand on each player on every play of every game whether on the field or in the dugout.

My coaching policy in this part of the season is to identify the strongest team possible to go with in the tournaments. I know a lot about baseball and I know a lot about motivating people. My task is to put those two knowledge bases together. Where I differ in philosophy from most coaches at this level is that I only think about today's game. As a matter of fact I have broken it down even further. I coach, as I played, one inning at a time. If you win the innings, the games take care of themselves.

Many coaches approach tournaments with a comprehensive plan to meet all of their opponents in order. They change their plan if unpredicted events occur, like upsets. I have seen coaches save pitchers or change a rotation to face a particular team. I'm not sophisticated enough to do that. I only play to win today. At this level of play, you have a one, two and three, etc. pitching staff. At age eighteen, everyone on the team knows it and believes in it as an approach. That fact alone makes me start them in order. I do reserve the option of going with a gut feeling at times but mostly I play the percentages. Since I can only play one inning at a time, I only think about one situation at a time. In sales it's called sell what's available today (SWAT).

The reality of gaining success is that you first have to become totally comfortable with yourself before you can begin concentrating on achieving it. This is as true in sports as it is in business. Each player has to become realistic about his strengths and recognize and define his limitations. On the surface we seem to have found the missing link needed to accept the responsibility and accountability of our respective roles on the team without losing our individuality. An analogy that can be made here is that of Rudyard Kipling in the <u>Jungle Book</u>; "The Power of the wolf is the pack, but the power of the pack is the wolf." The real strength of this team is the sum total of the strengths of all of the individual team members.

Our post-game talks become more analytical of how we played and what we need to work on. It is an exercise done to get every one involved and on the same page. Players start thinking in terms of what they can do to improve with each game.

Our next game is in St. Joseph, Michigan and Heyde is next in the rotation. We need a big game to demonstrate that we are on track. Schell hits two doubles and steals two bases setting the tone. Our iron man is up to it but it is hard to tell if the rest of the team is with him. Although Greg pitches a no hitter, two walks and three errors in the fifth inning give St. Joe three unearned runs after we had built a 4-0 lead. The rest of the game we are error free, as Greg retires six in a row. The 4-3 final is less than impressive. After the game we talk about it and everyone is measuring his role in it.

We try to practice everyday we don't play, but some days we need a break from one another. I try to be succinct on what we need to work on to make each practice more meaningful for every player. Here is where games are won – in practice! We're mainly working on the fundamentals. I don't want us to beat ourselves. In this beautifully simple game, more teams lose on mistakes than win because of big hits or home runs. Ironically players begin to see and suggest things that we need to practice on. This to me is a sign that they are beginning to tie our team's goals together with theirs.

In our next outing, we spot Buchanan, Michigan a 4-1 lead before our offense comes to life. Coker homers, Andert, Shepherd and Ross get two hits apiece to earn the 5-4 win. We're winning and almost everyone is contributing, but we still haven't arrived. My main concern is that we're spotting an opponent a lead before getting serious. This approach can really come back to haunt you.

Our arch rival, Post 357, poses our next challenge. While Hankins is only giving up five hits, our defense plays errorless ball including a double play and a putout at the plate. Madey calls a great game and adds two hits in the 4-0 shutout. Our confidence now seems to be growing so much that even I'm beginning to see it. Mr. Kouts' words, however, keep echoing in my ear "… I don't care if you don't beat anyone else as long as you beat Post 357". This game satisfies Mr. Kouts' expectations.

After disposing of Dowagiac, Michigan 5-1, we get to face Elkhart who had beaten us the first time we met. They promptly open the game by scoring 4 runs in the first inning and lead 5-1. Rudasics relieves Clarke striking out two to end the inning and leaves Elkhart with the basis loaded. Our offense again comes to life. Led by Vargyas and Heyde with two hits apiece, we score five runs in the last four innings to chalk up a 6-5 win. It is after this game that I suggest to the team that even though we have the talent and will to come from behind in every game it isn't necessary to prove it on a game-to-game basis.

Our final wins of this streak happen in Whiting, Indiana going again with Mike Clark and Jeff Rudasics, we beat a team that we might be seeing later in the year. We win both 4-0 and 6-2 respectively. Andert and Heyde get two hits each in the opener and Madey hits safely three times with Dan Szajko and Clarke contributing two each in the nightcap. This is a much more comfortable way to do it.

This seven-game run moves us to an overall record of 23 wins against only 6 losses. It seems that it was the team meeting after Elkhart beat us that was the catalyst to renew our resolve and opened the door for us to be able to take this inventory of ourselves and our motives. Our sense of urgency came from the fact that we only had those final games left before the sectional started to accomplish this transformation. We had been swimming up stream for the previous twelve games and we had no choice but to change our direction. Fortunately we were able to do it.

Bill and I review our personnel and come to an agreement on where we are with them and how to use them in the Sectional tournament. Our defense appears to be set. Bill Schell anchors the infield at short not only because of his skills and baseball knowledge but also because of the respect he commands from the other players. Jeff Coker is at third solidifying our left side of the infield. Gary Vargyas gives us a tough, passionate player at second base. We have used Jim Andert for the entire season at first and we feel that he has made a completely successful conversion. He'll bat second because he's patient, rarely strikes out and has great baseball instincts. We are more than comfortable with Romeo and Madey sharing the catching responsibilities and calling their own games and at this juncture they seem to be interchangeable. We have strong arms across the outfield. Mike Clarke in center field is backed up by Dan Szajko and we have Heyde and Yates in left and Shepherd in right field. That gives us four pitchers' arms in the outfield.

The pitching rotation is not yet set even though I consider Heyde and Hankins our co- number ones followed by Yates at number three. We also have Rudasics, Clarke, Shepherd and Kowatch to pitch if we need them. Our role players are Toles at first and Ross as our number three catcher.

Our batting order is indeed unique. I am able to have a 1,2,3 -1,2,3 - 1,2,3 order. Our first trio started with Bill Schell, the classic leadoff man. He hits for average has an unbelievable on base percentage and is the fastest and smartest runner we have on the bases. He is followed by Jim Andert who is a pure contact hitter with the patience of a saint giving Schell a chance to move on the bases. Jeff Coker, who provides us with proven game breaking power in the lineup, I move to the third spot from cleanup because I want him to come up more times in every game.

My middle trio of hitters consists of Mike Clarke, Will Shepherd and Greg Heyde. I started the year with Mike batting fourth, Will fifth and Heyde sixth but they appear to be interchangeable and they are just as effective. All three are contact hitters and are able to hit for power to all fields.

The final third of the order is led by Jeff Kowatch who was a leadoff man in high school. Whoever is catching, Madey or Romeo, is next followed by the pitcher, except Heyde because he is consigned to the middle trio. Then Szajko or Yates will step into the third trio and actually strengthen it. Even our role players usually bat in the place of whomever they replace. I now believe that we have our opponents at a disadvantage because we are so deep on offense and defense.

In my opinion, one of the most significant changes happens to Jeff Coker. His right of passage began when he returned to the team realizing that he needs to be playing with Post 50 rather than for it, as he waits to be signed. He needs to have a venue for the scouts to see him in action rather than just an on-field tryout. As we finish the final part of our season, he gets caught up in the excitement that we are beginning to generate. He not only wants to be a part of it but also is very aware that he has the skills to play a major role in determining the outcome.

Another key change is that Dave Hankins' self confidence has grown to the point where he is no longer afraid of making a mistake and with that comes the fun of playing the game again. He completely trusts his own skills and more importantly has come to trust the defensive team behind him completely. With these changes we are now ready to begin playing the tournament.

We are no longer the contingents from the four separate high schools who happen to be playing on the same team. Instead we have evolved into a single minded unit working toward a common goal of winning a championship. I can feel the change that has occurred with the team as a whole. I'm hungry to get started and test our lineups in actual tournament play.

BOTTOM OF THE 4TH

Time is an inexact concept in baseball. It is strange, sometimes very difficult to grasp. Some events for a baseball team seem to develop, over a period of time, rather than just happen during one day or game. Defining what was the key game or most important event, "the moment" that catapults a unit to their highest level of competing is sometimes easy to recognize, and then sometimes it is very difficult. For this team, maybe it was our team meeting after the Elkhart loss, maybe not. When exactly we got our "shtuff" together is difficult to pin down. My personal belief is that we just individually and then collectively decided that we each would do what was necessary to allow us to win the next game, and it snowballed into quite an impressive winning streak.

We were the best players on our collective high school teams. But it took a while for us to understand the nuances of becoming a true team with this collection of talent, fighting for each other and the group success. Appreciating each other and melding our games together took a while. The part that separates this team from other teams I had and have played on is very difficult to describe to people. It's not just talent, though obviously we had plenty of very good baseball players, with complete games, and not too many weaknesses. But I've played on, coached, and have seen other talented teams that weren't nearly as formidable as this team. Our team had strong individuals, mentally and physically. Don't confuse strength with size, especially in baseball. It's a mistake. We seemed to all know, individually, when to press the button for some juice, and when to relax and watch our teammates do their thing. It's like a concert where every section of the orchestra does their thing collectively, and for great songs, they each have solos from time to time that accentuate their excellent, unique talent. Once we found the right music, it was difficult to silence us. We were a cacophony of sorts in the beginning of our summer together…we transformed into a very harmonious symphony by the time the summer ended in New Hampshire.

We just finally reached the point where not one of us wanted to let the others down, because each of us was finally close enough to each other; as friends and as teammates. We weren't rival high school all-stars anymore scrambled together. We were defined in our minds now as teammates, representing each other and our community. That is critical for any group of athletes in a team game. And there is pressure involved in coming to that place emotionally. But all 17 of us were finally willing to give up the "I" part of our games for the most part, and give ourselves to the team success. Some teams and some players can never get there. The pressure of playing well all the time is too much. You still have to play well individually to pull off what we ended up doing, but it now wasn't the MOST important thing. We finally trusted each other's games enough. When you know you don't have to do it all, all the time, you can relax and let the game come to you a little, which is extremely important the higher you reach in terms of level of baseball.

We began to trust each other, in many different ways. But especially knowing that we were all giving it up, at all times on the field, was comforting. And that includes all the guys who weren't in the starting lineup. They were also key components, engaged in helping us win, however they could. We were the most complete team in that sense that I have ever been a part of. We all left it all on the field, and we knew that someone would always be able to put us over the top in the game we were playing at that time. We never knew who would be the guy for that day, but we had enough talent that we spread it around quite nicely.

It comes down again, in my opinion, to competitive maturity. I knew how competitive I was. Now I could sense that my teammates were at the same place. We poured competitive instinct from every fiber of our beings from the Elkhart loss to New Hampshire like no team I have ever seen or been a part of. But when that level of focus specifically occurred is hard to pinpoint. It probably happened at different times for different players. And for those that happened to catch this feeling early, they could coax the others into joining them as we went along, like a wet snowball rolling downhill...by the bottom of the hill it is a formidable piece of nature.

After the Elkhart loss, we spent the next couple of weeks engaged in saying YES to southern Michigan communities and teams, and defeating upcoming Sectional and Regional opponents, including our

South Bend rival, Post 357. They were all good teams and the most important win was a rematch with Elkhart that we won 6-5. We won seven games in a row and had some nice momentum heading into the state tournament. It was a feeling that started to grow little by little. Our defense and pitching came together so well at the end of our regular season, that our confidence started to get to the point of expecting to play well all of the time. Offensively we were tough from the top of the order all the way through number nine. Our confidence in each other and the fun we were starting to have with each other both on and off the field was putting us in a very comfortable position, a position of wanting to test ourselves every night, every game, against anyone who wanted a piece of us. Not all teams reach that as a complete unit. Sometimes it's just the exceptional players on a team that reach that place. With our team it was everyone and it empowered us, collectively, as well as individually.

We enjoyed watching each other make great plays. Sometimes teammates take that for granted. They don't actually see the grace and skill needed to do the things that make people catch their breath. They of course like to watch it, but they can't embrace the fact that they are witnessing something very special from others. If all you've ever done on a baseball field is play for yourself, your stats, and the spotlight; what others do, even on your own team, has little effect upon you.

Aggressiveness was also a key part of our transformation. We were really taking it to our opponents at this point of the season. We weren't blowing people away by 10 runs all the time, but we weren't giving them a chance by never giving up a big inning on defense. That was our staple all the way through this period and tournament run. We never caved, neither the pitchers, nor the defense. When you can't score many runs, it's difficult to build any momentum. Our team found out that momentum in baseball can also be found on defense and the pitcher's mound.

We were starting to run on all eight cylinders, literally. Our team was fast and quick. We forced people out of their comfort zones with our offensive philosophy. We stole bases, took the extra base, and made the defense always have to worry. That relentless pressure took its toll psychologically on our opponents. It made them sometimes play a little quick and caused errors, both physical and mental. We made them pay for those mistakes too. Though you still have to get to first base obviously, and we did that consistently.

We had many players who were really playing well offensively during this stretch of games. We never did strike out much at all. We made a lot of contact up and down our lineup. We had one true power hitter, the best I've ever played with, and many who could also hit it long once in a while. We hit many doubles, and more triples than most teams because of our speed. There were no easy outs, no matter who Mel played. And we were versatile. Our batting lineup rarely changed with the exception of the four, five, and six holes. Mel had a unique way of looking at our offense and by this point in the summer had a good idea of what players could do. Shepherd, Heyde, and Clarke would be the ones who would have to look at the lineup card before the games. Everyone else knew where he would hit, depending upon who was pitching. Mel also had a great feel for who should bat cleanup behind Coker. If I was hot, it would be me. If Gregg was having good at bats, Mel would choose him. And batting sixth for Mel on this team is like hitting in the three hole. When the players in front of you are always on base, you get plenty of RBI opportunities. Mike always seemed to make great contact and moved runners along, so he was a good candidate for the five or six hole also. We were getting results from everyone at different times and it made for some long days and nights for our opponents.

Looking back, I think what was fun for Mel was the fact that we could beat teams in so many different ways. We had more versatility than any team I've seen for that age group, period. And as our coach, he controlled for the most part, which assortment of weapons to use for that particular challenge. If he sensed defensive weakness in our opponents we played small ball and ran a lot. If he felt the pitcher was not strong enough, he played first and third offense all night. Mel always paid close attention to the pitcher's stretch habits and the talent and arm of the opposing catcher. Whatever it took. He seemed to know what buttons to push for each game and opponent. We were the kind of team that the current Oakland A's represent to people in today's pro game. Not high dollar super stars but players who could get results and were consistent. We did the little things that matter, on a daily basis. We certainly didn't beat ourselves.

I read the book by the Oakland A's general manager, Billy Bean, titled Money Ball. Too bad he wasn't around when we played. We were the kind of guys he would seriously look at as prospects. Our size wouldn't be held against us so much. Production is what he and others in professional baseball really care about now. How much do you add to the team's winning? In what ways? The categories and stats that impress clubs now are a little different. They will always look for the five tool guys, those guys are easy to spot and scout. But more and more baseball people now see what really wins games. He and other young GM's are training their scouts and development people to look for the players that make the difference between winning and losing over the long haul, the people that make it happen week in and week out. And that isn't always the 3-run HR hitters, or guys who steal 80 bases. Balance, athleticism, plate discipline, on base percentage, maturity, position versatility, and mental toughness are much more in vogue now than in 1977. Those were some of our strengths. If you were not the right size for your position back when we played, forget it.

Our mindset for the start of the tournament was pretty good. We were playing well and we were becoming much closer to the team Mel had envisioned we could become at the start of the summer. Pitching was very good with Hank and Heyde leading the way. But we were also getting good innings from others, Yates and Rudy especially, and that was important heading into the state tournament. We had really done quite well considering that Jano hadn't pitched for us yet (an Indiana North All-Star), and Mike Clarke's shoulder problems kept him from being a mainstay for us. Defense was getting more solid it seemed. We never did give up many runs, and during this phase we stayed true to form. Offensively we had many players hitting well consistently. Our catching was very good also. We had confidence in whomever Mel put back behind the plate. They would keep the ball in front of them and give us a chance. We didn't give up free bases very much.

Our regular season record was 23 – 6. We were playing well and enjoying each other, and having fun. I, and I believe my team-mates, were only worried about the game that day. Our approach and mental state at this time of transition were solid. Someone would have to play a complete game to beat us. At this point we were developing many ways to defeat opponents. Whatever was needed, we seemed to come up with.

We were developing a resiliency that I haven't seen to this day. We were tested by quality opponents during this stretch of games. Our level of consistency was becoming one of our strengths. Our mid-to-late game comebacks and consistent defense and pitching were taking form now. We were definitely improving in many different areas that are critical to overall success on a baseball field. The team's confidence was becoming palpable. We knew the state tournament would be competitive. Our area of Northern Indiana had a ton of talent to go around. Teams would test us, we knew that going in. But we were ready for the challenge.

RUDASICS #8
I remember coming in against Elkhart in the first inning in relief of Mike Clarke (they already had four runs). I had just gotten out of the car and could hear Mel telling me to hurry up and get loose. I put my cleats on and within minutes I was in the game. I struck out the first two guys and got out of a bases loaded jam. It may

have been my most memorable moment. I kept us in the game and Heyde came in relief the last two innings to get the win.

ANDERT #7
Guys like Coker, Shepherd, Schell, Heyde, Hankins and Szajko... well I think you get my point. All had natural instincts and abilities for the game while I had to struggle mightily to hold my own and not let my teammates down.

KOWATCH #1
Sitting the bench most of the summer, the first in my athletic career, was a great learning experience for me. Most importantly, it taught me the principle, to be faithful to the task given me. If taking infield is my "play" for that day, do it as well as I could. If it were warming up an outfielder between innings, do that as well as I could for that teammate.

TOLES #9
There was a quiet optimism and confidence that grew during the entire regular season; a comfort level with each other that is a part of every championship team. Mel nurtured this and guided it, but most importantly, challenged it. He made us understand that it was okay to play for our team and ourselves, not for the coach or our parents. We learned to trust him and each other.

That was his gift to us. The next eighteen games would be our gift to him!

5TH INNING

Indiana Tournament

"Ready or not here we come!"

TOP OF THE 5TH

The team that represents South Bend Post 50 in the Tournaments in August of the 1977 season is not the same team we started the season with in June. Most of the players are the same but important changes have occurred in each player who stayed. Although you would think that these changes would happen insidiously, they actually happened at a pace that no coach could have planned or even hoped to realize. They happened over one-half of a single season. It became clear to me as I worked with them that the main concept I had to get across to them was and is that success is not an endpoint but a mode of travel. This message which is so simple to state is difficult to adopt and inculcate into your daily on the field actions.

In Indiana, the state tournament has three tournament levels. The sectional is the first level with all of the local teams participating. The winners move on to the Regionals which quarter the state and the four Regional winners plus a host team then play in the State Finals. Each level is double elimination.

After finishing the regular season as we did on a 7-0 run, we find a new level of confidence. This Sectional Tournament is scheduled in the newest of the city's ball diamonds, Belleville Park, which is located at the western edge of South Bend seemingly in the country because a cornfield runs along the center and right field fences. It does have stands and a permanent press box and a rest room building. We use the park department's diamonds because we don't have our own.

Our true measure of preparedness, however, is about to be tested in the form of Elkhart Post 74, the last team to defeat us during the regular season. Elkhart is as competitive a team as we could face and even though we came back to beat them the second time we played (6-5), they are totally unimpressed with us.

Our first game in this tournament has an inauspicious beginning. It's a hard fought game that is officially termed a forfeit even though we are winning 6-4 when the deciding incident occurs. The newspaper account describes it this way; ..."Although his own throwing errors cost him two runs, the Elkhart pitcher, Jim Heeg, still had a no hitter working against Post 50 when arm trouble forced him out in the eighth inning following a walk and another throwing error on Bill Schell's bunt." After the pitching change to Mark Salee, an infield hit by Andert, Post 50's first hit, a sacrifice fly by Mike Clarke and a monstrous home run by Coker, gave us a total of four runs in the inning. What happened next was ugly. After a Gary Vargyas triple, Will Shepherd hit a ground ball back to Salee and Vargyas should have been an easy out at the plate, but Vargyas came in high and took out the catcher. "...the scuffle that followed triggered an ugly pushing, shoving and shouting scene that involved umpires, players and Elkhart fans." At that point Elkhart's coach pulled their team off the field and the game was called. At the time we were winning 6-4.

I know that I have to calm my team down after this game. I have to make sure that we are playing under control. I'm not about to let an incident like this set the tone for the entire tournament. I can't let any of them celebrate what has just happened. I do however emphasize that we are in the winner's bracket and moving on to our second game because we came from behind and were playing an inning at a time per our game plan.

Our next game places us against our arch rival South Bend Post

357. This is an important game because the players all know each other and also know that on any given day either team can win regardless of our respective records. The rivalry is repeatedly put into perspective by our baseball chairman, Bob Kout's, enduring statement, "I don't care how many games you win or lose as long as you beat Post 357." Last year our team eliminated Post 357 from post season tournament play by beating them twice in the South Bend Sectional, a particular sore spot since they had won the state championship in 1975 and had most of their team back. Their 1977 team is relatively new but again they are as deep in talent as any of the other teams we meet in northern Indiana.

As the South Bend Tribune reported it, "Post 357 took a 2-0 lead in the fourth inning against Post 50 as Larry Zielinski tripled home a run and scored on Mark Witucki's second double. But Post 50 tied it in the sixth, then scored in every inning the rest of the way ..." The story continued, "Jeff Coker blasted a home run into the street beyond the left field fence in the eighth, his second homer of the tournament." This posts our second come-from-behind victory in as many games. This team is beginning to believe that we are going to score as many runs as it takes to beat whomever we play. We have all three of the necessary components, hitting, pitching and defense.

Our third and fourth victories of the sectional tournament come at the expense of Michigan City, a team that had beaten us 4-0 in our own July 4th Holiday Tournament when we were at our low point of our season. As stated earlier, we are not the same team in this tournament that we were on the 4th of July. We have gone through a metamorphosis in attitude and focus. We eliminate Michigan City 15-0 and 14-2., I'm not sure that they know what just hit them. This solidifies our new posture in our minds and in the minds of most of our fans which, at this point, are still mainly friends and families.

The Regional Tournament is also played in South Bend but this tournament is at Kennedy Park, the oldest park in the city.

Advancing from the northwest corner of the state are teams from Whiting, Hammond and Crown Point.

Crown Point, our first opponent sports an impressive 18-8 record. Although we have extended our winning streak to 11 games, in my mind I need to have a contrasting pitcher, one who will completely change our look on the mound. This will be even more important later in the tournament against a team who may be a fastball-hitting team. Since we don't have a left hander, the only thing we can add is a curve ball pitcher. Dennis Janiszewski, who broke his finger in the third game of the year but hasn't missed a game or practice while he was recuperating, is that pitcher. This is a good time to use him since all of our other pitchers have all 12 innings of their eligibility left. If he gets into trouble, he has lots of help in the bullpen.

Dennis is so ready, he can taste it. This is his chance to come back. Jano, as everyone calls him, gives us seven strong innings. He strikes out seven and walks only one and limits Crown Point to only five hits. Our defense and hitting greatly help his confidence. Mike Clarke has a three-hit day and Will Shepherd blasts a three-run homer that takes the pressure off. Heyde, in relief, completes the final two innings to give us an 8-2 win. Something we sorely need, a contrast pitcher, is back!

The team is visibly coming together and everyone can see it. More fans are showing up to watch us play. Next up is Whiting. With the score tied at 1, it is Will Shepherd's bat again that breaks it open with another three-run homer, his second in two games. Meanwhile, Dave Hankins is giving us a superb effort giving up only five hits and striking out twelve. With his slider working he has them all off stride except for their first baseman, Ken Kalima, who has a three-hit day including a solo home run. The final is 5-1 and we move on to the championship game.

Whiting advances through the loser's bracket and now they have to face our other ace, Greg Heyde. The results are strikingly similar. Against Greg they score two runs on eight hits and two errors but Heyde keeps their scoring in check with 11 strikeouts.

On offense we get eleven hits and five walks with the big blow, a solo homer in the sixth, coming again from Shepherd for his third in three regional games. Everyone now thinks that Will is either possessed by some supernatural power or his undershirt has a big S on it. We win the Regional Tournament in three games.

Our next stop, Richmond, Indiana, a town located on east I-70 halfway between Columbus, OH and Indianapolis, is the sight of the Indiana American Legion State Finals. This is our first on-the-road tournament. I have been predicting all year that we would win the State Championship and now the opportunity has truly arrived and we have to prove it. The field is an old minor league baseball park situated near the middle of the city. It has covered stands and 90-feet-high night lights and an inner cyclone fence surrounded by a solid green wooden fence that forms an almost perfect square from backstop to outfield fence. In the left field section there is a hill or at least elevated ground that runs from the third base line street parallel to the outer left field fence to the center field corner of the stadium. The original field was oversized but has been shorted by the inner cyclone fence that was added many years later. A singular sign which labels the distance from home plate to left field near that center field corner reads 497 feet in large yellow numbers is a statement to its size. This is a distance too far even to think about reaching since Comiskey Park in Chicago has a center field fence only 405 feet from home plate.

In mid July we had swept a double header from a Terre Haute team in South Bend. Now we get to play against the other Terre Haute team in our first game of the tournament that evening at 8pm. This team is stronger and has the elite left handed pitcher of the tournament and probably the entire state, John Newman.

Jano starts in the first game of this tournament for the same reason I used him in the first game of the regional, if his arm isn't ready I still have the rest of the pitching staff with all twelve innings of eligibility left. There is no doubt about it, John Newman, is the best we have seen so far this year. He strikes out fourteen of us and appears to be in complete control of the game. On offense,

Terre Haute bunches three hits in the first inning but is only able to score one run. Jano's arm isn't what it was against Crown Point and in the third inning it really starts to give him trouble. To relieve him, I bring in Heyde, who started in left field. He is spectacular, giving up only two hits in six scoreless innings of relief. Meanwhile on offense, Dan Szajko who replaced Heyde in left goes three for three and Andert and Coker each get two hits. But the big surprise comes in the bottom of the eighth when Romeo sends a frozen rope over the 330-foot mark landing on the terrace outside the left field fence. The final score is South Bend 5 and Terre Haute 1.

Conventional wisdom earmarks Lafayette Post 11, as the favorite going into this tournament and they live up to that billing against us. Rob Burgess holds us hitless until the fourth inning when Coker singles to left. From that point on we are able to apply constant pressure by virtue of eight hits and five walks. On the mound for us, Hankins has a rocky inning in the third when he gives up three of their five hits and they are able to score three runs. After that Dave takes a deep breath, tightens his belt and retires the next 13 hitters in a row. For our side we score one in the fifth on Schell's single to knock in Szajko who had doubled with two out. Trailing 3-1 in the seventh, we bat around scoring three runs and take the lead at 4-3. That inning opens with Romeo taking one for the team, followed by four singles and a ground-rule double by Shepherd knocking in Coker with the lead run. Then Hankins, with some defensive help, closes them out the final two innings for the win.

It is after this game that the team truly believes that we are going to win the championship. This is proven by the fact that they decided to celebrate, albeit a game early. We have returned to the hotel and Dan Szajko approaches me and asks if I have anything in my wallet that shouldn't get wet. He catches me off guard and before I know what's happening I am gang tackled by the team and thrown into the swimming pool. Mr. Barcome closely follows. Bill always follows me everywhere when we are playing on the road.

With our 4-3 win over Lafayette, we move on to the championship game. Lafayette can't believe the loss to us and is noticeably angry after our game. They bombard Beech Grove in the loser's bracket game 19-3 to get another shot at us. Parenthetically, Beech Grove is the team that swept us in a double header on our Indianapolis trip on July 2nd. We know we're in for a fight.

I call on Dave Yates to start but the Lafayette team is still working on the adrenalin from their Beech Grove win and they are ready for us. Dave, who at 6' 5" is our biggest player and hardest thrower, has a steaming fast ball. After Dave strikes out their leadoff hitter and retires their number two man, Lafayette jumps all over him with four singles, and a walk making it 4-0. At this point, I can either bring out a white flag or Dave Hankins who had three innings of eligibility left to try to end the inning. I choose Hankins who they promptly attack for an RBI single to give them their fifth run before their leadoff man mercifully flies out to end the inning.

I later found out that the Beech Grove pitchers that Lafayette had just pounded threw almost as hard as Yates. I should have started a contrasting pitcher and brought Dave in for relief. This would have been more effective against this type of team.

We have to regroup! This is going to take some planning. Yates couldn't be re-entered, Hankins had two and two thirds innings left, Heyde only had six innings left and Jano's arm was hurting. I looked at Dave Hankins and said, "Can you stop them?"

"Yes. I can!" he responded with little or no emotion.

"Okay then, you'll have to give me what you have left and then Heyde you're going to have to finish it for us."

In the top of the 2nd Hankins gets them out three up and three down.

"We need one run this inning. We can't wait!" I say on my way out to the third base coaching box as we come up to bat. It turns out better than I asked for. After a walk and an error, Bill Schell triples to the right field wall and we put two on the board.

Hankins gets three up and three down again in the third. In the fourth somebody is calling my name from the stands, it's Mr. Hankins, Dave's dad, reminding me that Dave can only pitch for two outs this inning and is worried that if a man gets on and a double play possibility occurs that may take him over his eligibility. In explanation, I calm him down assuring him that double and triple plays are the exception to the eligibility rule and we are okay if that happens. In the fourth, Dave gets the first two hitters out to complete his eligibility. Heyde follows and pitches to only one batter to end the inning. I can see a calm confidence taking the place of some of the earlier anxiety.

If we're going to do it, it has to be now. In the fifth inning Schell singles to start the inning and with one out Coker hits a shot, that shouldn't have landed yet, absolutely stunning the crowd. It explodes off of his bat and hits the triangle atop the center field light standard that stands about 90 feet off the ground. People were rubbing their eyes in disbelief. After what seemed like an eternity of silent solemnity as Jeff rounds the bases, Heyde comes up. Greg follows with a line drive that clears the left field fence tying the score at 5. Now it's our game.

Their futility at the plate coupled with our tying the score has more than just a negative effect on them; it seems to completely deflate them. On our side we are relentless, as we continued to hold them hitless since the first inning, we keep pressure on them on the bases. Coker singles and scores the lead run in the seventh. In the eighth we score an insurance run when Schell steals second after getting his third hit. They decide to intentionally walk Coker and as the pitcher lobs ball four to Coker, Schell steals third. As the demoralized defense is staring at Schell, Coker steals second. This is followed by Shepherd knocking in Schell on a grounder to third. In the three games in Richmond Coker has 7 hits in 9 at bats.

To recap the game; following the first inning hit off Hankins, he and Heyde hold Lafayette hitless and scoreless the rest of the game. Finally, one thing seems certain, our pitching is set now with Heyde, Hankins, Jano and Yates. There is no doubt in anybody's mind that we are the State Champions and for our part we have achieved our primary goal.

Having said that, what happened to our team in the Indiana State Tournament is very revealing. It began in the Sectional and ended in the Finals. How our team performed is like Ravel's "Bolero". We became a study in crescendo, not letting the things we couldn't do interfere with the things we could do. We just kept doing them over and over again, getting stronger each time.

After the award ceremony, we're told to go home and wait; we have eight days to rest and pack. Transportation will be arranged for us and we have to be in Chicago by next Tuesday to represent Indiana in the Great Lakes Regional.

BOTTOM OF THE 5TH

Sectional: Bellville and Kennedy Parks, South Bend, Indiana

Our offense cranked it up a couple of notches for our sectional championship. We were scoring a bunch of runs against our opponents, the pitching and defense remained solid, and our competitive attitudes helped us to repeat as South Bend Sectional Champions without much difficulty. Our only hiccup was in our very first game against Elkhart, a game that we could have easily lost. We had to come back against them, and it started a tendency of late inning rallies that we would rely on at critical junctures for the rest of the state and national tournaments. Jeff Coker hit a massive home run late in the game (8th inning). He was really playing well and hitting some shots for us, but we were kind of used to it by now. Expected it really. V had a collision at home plate with their catcher and scored a crucial run for us. Ball went flying, catcher went flying, and V was wondering who picked up the fumble and scored. Elkhart protested the play, then decided to forfeit, and just walked out at that point. The protest was not upheld by tournament officials and we got our first win of the tournament.

The next couple of games were offense at its finest. We crushed our rival, Post 357, and enjoyed every minute of that. Everyone

72

was hitting and running, and we just rolled. It became a chain reaction kind of thing. Everyone got into the act.

We smoked Michigan City in back-to-back games to win the championship, but it still to this day bothers us that they were the ONLY team the entire season to shut us out; 4-0, back in our July 4th Tournament. We obviously had found ourselves and from that terrible day and game, a much different team was what they experienced in the sectional. The message was clear though to everyone in Northern Indiana. We were for real, and we were starting to get Big Mo rolling.

Regional: Kennedy Park, South Bend, Indiana

The only home run hit against our pitching staff at any level of the tournament occurred in the state regional. Ken Kalima from Whiting hit one in the second game. It didn't do too much damage, in that game, or to our psyche. We took care of business and defeated teams from the Region (Northwest Indiana) to advance to our goal all along, the State Championship. To have done it in front of our families and friends made it that much more special.

I was seeing the ball well and hit home runs in each of our three games. I am most proud of the second one as I called it in the dugout beforehand, much to the amusement and/or disgust of some of my teammates. When I took the first pitch curve ball out for another three run homer...well, you can imagine the crap I caught from the Bad News Bears. I had called first pitch, first pitch curve ball, and my semi-classic home run trot also. They couldn't stand it. Dizzy Dean said it best, "It ain't braggin if you can back it up".

What also was fun for me though was the next night when I hit a solo shot against Whiting in our championship game. As I rounded second I saw Mel and his grin. I always liked that grin, a lot, and you didn't have to hit a home run to see it. He grins a lot. Nice personality trait for a youth baseball coach, don't you think? He held up three fingers against his stomach. Right after giving him five, I looked up and about 10 ft. or so from Mel, standing almost on the chalk line was Bill Schell. The rest of our team surrounded the home plate area. What Bill said to me was priceless and also on the money, "Someone pinch this clown and wake him up from the dream"! It cracked me up. We're headed to state and I had another new position, second base. V had to report to Purdue for football practice so our second baseman would miss the state finals.

Now our focus could really be on the prize. We all remembered Mel's references to winning the state championship on the first day we were all together, and after our 4th of July Tournament loss to Michigan City. We now had our opportunity; the opportunity to prove Mel prophetic, and to prove to Northern Indiana people and the entire state that we were the best team around.

State Finals: Richmond, Indiana

Now we were on the road for the first time in a long time. Destination: Richmond, Indiana and the State Finals. The sectional and regional were played in South Bend, which made it convenient and nice for our families and fans. Familiar surroundings made it real nice to win the first two parts of the state tournament. What we now knew was that the competition level would definitely increase in Richmond. Lafayette had a good team. Lafayette Jeff High School had been ranked very high in the state baseball rankings for a number of years, and this year they had another very good team, and with the addition of some other area players, no one was surprised that they came to the state finals with an impressive record. We also were familiar with the Beech Grove team, and their appearance surprised no one on our team. Terre Haute had a highly ranked team in high school that spring, so they weren't a surprise either. We were poised for a very competitive state championship experience.

This opportunity meant different things for each of us. For the Clay guys, it would have to be the state championship they barely missed out on the year before in high school baseball. For the rest of us, it would validate our talent and skill levels. And for the returnees, it would be a chance to make up for last summer at Kokomo. I can't speak for Mel and the coaching staff, but I believe this would also prove to themselves and others that you can win big doing it the right way. So we all had a lot to prove, to ourselves, and to the rest of the baseball people in the state.

At this point of the late summer, college plans were starting to become a distraction of sorts for some of us. I remember my thinking all along was that college could wait. There was REAL serious business to attend to: baseball. I was only thinking about the game, my position change from left field to second base, and what I needed to do to help us win the title. For others, the timing of the tournament games and these college plans were starting to get a little messy.

In our first game, against Terre Haute, was the moment I became completely convinced we were a special team. We face this lefty who struck us out 14 times. Unthinkable! I would have lost the house betting on someone doing that to our lineup. I think he got me twice. Nasty, nasty stuff! John Newman was his name. He pitched for some outstanding Indiana State University teams. This just in...he was pretty good! You couldn't see the ball until it's on you, and just when you got semi-locked into his sneaky fastball, he dropped a late breaking curve ball on you that seemed to start somewhere near our dugout. You naturally gave up on it and at the last second it came dipping into the strike zone. His stuff was some of the toughest we saw in the whole tournament.

Anyway, Dom Romeo, our #9 hitter, takes one of those nasty curves, which was in and on his shoe tops it seemed to me, not even a strike, and literally golfed it right down the left field line in the eighth inning for a big time "Welcome to the State Finals Dominic" home run. Good thing. It was getting late and we needed to break a few hearts to really feel like we had accomplished something that day. This guy had made many of us look extremely bad for eight innings, including Dom, but the Italian pretty boy woke everyone up with one funky sand wedge. Unbelievable! We didn't know much about Dom's history as a hitter but suffice it to say that he wasn't labeled as much of a power guy. As soon as it came off his bat you knew it was gone...into the dark foggy night.

I would love for all of us to see those few moments of his life again, not just to see the ball get lost over the fence and the dejection on the faces of our opponents, but to see his face again as he rounded second and third. It was special, for him, and for us. To a man, right there and then, and not saying it out loud to anyone, I believe we all were wondering if we weren't just a little special.

It was a statement home run, the kind that every team needs from time to time. It came from an unexpected source, your new guy, the #9 hitter. Dom hadn't played very many games with us to this point, and we had never seen him hit a ball that hard and far. It gave you a confidence that's critical for a team. You were never out of a game, because you never knew who would deliver you from a tight spot. The bottom of our order had guys that could hit, run, steal bases, bunt, and drive runs in. There truly was no drop off in production. They always were helping us win games with key plays on both offense and defense.

Another clear memory for me in that game occurred real late when our shortstop, Bill Schell, was stealing third base. I believe the score was tied or maybe we were one run ahead. The curve ball was in the dirt and got away from their catcher. He hustled to retrieve it near the backstop. The pitcher was moving to cover the plate just in case Schell tried the unthinkable play by trying to score. Without even a thought of slowing down, Bill turned the corner at third and motored toward the plate. He scored a huge run for us, and it wasn't even close at the plate. Mel just watched, like we all did, as Bill hit fifth gear. I wasn't sure if he even had to slide.

I just remember thinking to myself at that very moment two things: 1. Only a handful of players that I ever played with or against would even consider being that aggressive. 2. Damn, I sure am glad he's on my team. It's the kind of play that has stuck in my mind forever because it was and is the kind of play that will win you a big game or a championship, and did. It takes the heart out of your opponent, at crunch time. It also gave our team a feeling that's difficult to describe to people. It's not total invincibility, but it was real close. Your best and fastest player forcing the pitcher to not put it in the dirt, or to not make a key mistake because we would take advantage of every opportunity. For a lefty like Newman, a nasty curve in the dirt was a tremendous weapon that he was used to using - a punch out pitch. Bill took that play completely away from him. Now he had to throw strikes, or at least pitches that we could do something with. The momentum shift was felt by everyone in the stadium, including our opponents. No hesitation. No doubt. No fear.

Also in that game, Dan Szajko had started to steal second twice or three times maybe and two of those times he got close to half way and came diving back into first, barely ahead of the middle infielder's throw back to first. Newman had one of those cheater's moves to first, he mixed it up with the front leg and head movement real well, and I'm sure Dan was wired for 220, so he was like a ping pong ball between first and second and had everyone with their hearts in their throats. Dan was very fast and a heads up base runner usually, but this wasn't your usual lefty where you could take off on first movement. The game was real tight and he didn't want to make a big bonehead out with the score close, real late in a nail biter. As for me, I didn't want to make my teammates nervous about me getting picked off first, so I don't remember ever reaching first base safely in that game. Great late-game heroics by a number of guys, I just didn't happen to be one of them.

In our second game against Lafayette, I hit one of my 7 irons to left-center off of their ace, an All-Stater named Rob Burgess, who later pitched for Purdue University. He was 6'7" and a very good athlete, and had really good stuff. I was thinking that I got all of it. I did…it's just that the fence in left-center in Richmond, Indiana was too far back. Much too far back; but not for Romeo and Heyde. I needed to talk to someone there about that. It bounced over for a ground rule double and I was thinking I got robbed. Mel said to me after the inning, "Too bad we weren't at Kennedy or you could have shown us that jog again". As for the folks in Richmond that day, they didn't get to see my home run trot.

In the championship game against Lafayette, Jeff Coker hit a monster shot; no, a tape measure job against this other pitcher. He put it about three quarters of the way up the light tower in center and as he crossed the plate he gave me five, looked me square in the eye and said, "...Do the same thing". Yeah Jeff, I would have done it, if you had let me hit the ball three times, run up and take the distance each time. It made my double the day before look like T-Ball practice. Trying to keep up with the Jeff Coker Show was just too much to deal with. It remains to this very day the most majestic and farthest traveling center field home run I have ever seen hit by a teenager, and I've coached high school baseball for over 20 years. The light tower was between, but way back from the current home run fence and the hill and the old minor league wood fence that was on top of the hill (which seemed and was marked at about 500 ft. from the plate). I'm scared and embarrassed to do the math. On second thought...I can't even DO the math he hit it so far and high. The entire crowd just went silent, as did we all. Everyone just watched it...Some fans were still trying to catch their breath and rationalize if what they saw was truly what they saw. It was. I saw it too, and had the best seat in the house for it. And I, unlike the nine guys on defense, didn't receive a broken neck watching him launch his space shuttle. No one could do it justice with just words. You had to see it.

I have some great pictures of our guys receiving their individual state championship trophies. The smiles were sincere. The hand shakes were firm and the eye contact with Mel was poignant. We had started this journey in early June and we had accomplished our goal. It wasn't easy, but it definitely was earned. Hank and Heyde had pitched their tails off in Richmond. Coker, Schell, and Szajko were on base all the time and had outstanding tournaments. Everyone played a part in our success though. It was a total team effort. We needed everyone's contributions. We had no idea what was next. We didn't really care at that point. We really weren't thinking of anything but enjoying our triumph. It even sounded as good as it felt…"State Champions".

YATES #10
In actual game experiences I had been someone who did a little pitching, a little designated hitting with an occasional game in the outfield. Being one of the younger guys on the team I was happy to contribute however and whenever I could. As the season went on I became more comfortable and really started to gain confidence in myself. Pitching in two sectional games and then getting called on to start the state championship game were definitely my highlights.

MADEY #12
Yates just looked really big out there, how big was he - 6'5"? He had a big old windup and a straight over the top delivery that was scary. His fast ball jumped left and right as it came in. He also had a good hard breaker to offset the fastball and like the rest of the staff, he had good control.

ANDERT #7
It was here that Bill Schell introduced me to the joys of putting a pinch of Skoal between my cheek and gum. What he did not tell me was the importance of not swallowing any. From that point it was a quick decline from dizziness, to queasy stomach, to palpitating bowels and finishing up with full-bore retching. How Bill could chew this crap and still be the best shortstop I have ever seen still baffles me.

COKER #19

The most shocking game memory I have is when Dom Romeo launched a missile into the fog in Richmond, IN. I had played with Dom since Little League and don't ever remember his going deep. Not only was that home run a game saver for us, but it was hit off a left hander, John Newman, who tallied 14 strikeouts against us and pretty much dominated us most of the night until Romeo "Dom"-inated that ankle high pitch. Good job, Dom.

TOLES #9

Immediately, after we won the state, I think that most of us thought we would go back home, regroup a little, bask in our 15 minutes of fame, go to Chicago, play a few more games, get our asses handed to us by someone, come home and go on about our lives.

I think that lasted until we actually started heading to Chicago. It was then that we understood someone was going to win this tournament and it might as well be us! Why not? The state tournament had shown us what we were. The National tournament was going to show us what we could be.

PITCHING STAFF:
Dave Hankins, Dennis Janiszewski, Jeff Rudasics, Greg Heyde, Dave Yates

6TH INNING

Great Lakes Regional

"The Unforgiving Minute"

TOP OF THE 6TH

It has been a long weekend, and the trip home from Richmond is a long five hour ride but somehow it isn't tiring. There is a feeling of satisfaction about winning the State Championship that I told them about the first week of practice. We now have some time to rest our pitchers, collect our thoughts and get prepared for our next tournament.

I tell the team, "Take tomorrow off and we'll practice the rest of the week."

There is way too much to think about; my mind is racing. I still have three days of vacation left and we're only going to Chicago to play and that's closer than Richmond. I know I have to call my boss and let him know where I am. He asks me how long I'll be gone and I tell him that we will probably lose the first two games and we'd be done by Thursday of next week. He congratulates me and says, "... Call me when you're done I'd like to take you to dinner."

Later that week, I receive a phone call from, Taxi Ayres, the Department (State) of Indiana Baseball Chairman, telling me that our transportation to the Great Lakes Regional in Chicago, is arranged and we will be picked up in South Bend and travel by chartered bus to Chicago with the Mansfield, Ohio team, the Ohio

State Champions. The Ohio team's head coach is Jim Mazeroski, who is a brother to Bill Mazeroski, the Pittsburgh Pirate who hit the home run against the New York Yankees to win the Major League World Series in 1960.

We are slated to arrive in Chicago on Tuesday because we have to attend the banquet where the main speaker is Ernie Banks. The hair on the back of my neck stands up. Talk about baseball, everything about this tournament is baseball, the stuff of which dreams are made. We are told that the participants in the Great Lakes Regional are the State Champions from Kentucky, Ohio, Indiana, Michigan, Illinois, Wisconsin plus a very strong host team with an impressive record. My competitive side says this is the place to be.

For my part, I am living a dream but there are other perspectives beginning to unfold. This "Once in a lifetime" phrase suddenly becomes the here and now. I am already running into obstacles; college orientations, college baseball seasons, vacations, and parents who feel that taking their children out of town and staying in a hotel with "literally no supervision" is not in their best interest. This last one is the easiest to overcome because of the American Legion Tournament rules of conduct. I'm sure you've heard the phrase, "It's my way or the highway!"

Seeing how the National Regional Tournament is conducted is a flashback to my military days. It is a first for the players. The military regimentation is evident. The teams are provided with two meals at the hotel and receive a daily food allowance, five two dollar bills per day for dinner. We are told when to eat and when we are on our own. We are provided with bus transportation, an escort or guide and an itinerary which has to be followed. The itinerary provided us with a list of rules including tournament and conduct rules plus a daily schedule that is non-negotiable along with a practice and game schedule. These don't appear to have a negative impact on our players who seemed to be content with just being here.

I am beginning to realize, however, that the parents, many of whom are first time college parents, are more nervous than the players about their son's being in this tournament. College suddenly becomes a safe haven far away from the pressures that the parents are feeling about their sons playing in this tournament. The mothers' statements ranged from "They are already State Champions, what more do they need to accomplish in one season?" What if we win at this level? How long will it go on?" " If my child misses his college orientation, he'll fail in college and subsequently in life!" The fathers are easier to deal with than the mothers because it is at this point that they become the liaisons. They are identifying with the success their sons are having which makes it easier to rationalize their son's participation, even if they are a little late for their college orientation.

From another perspective, parents see their children as only they can. This may have been their way of alleviating the angst that they are feeling about their child when we reached this level. They don't see infielders, outfielders, pitchers or catchers. They only see their sons as the little boys they raised. They see them as fallible human beings they know and love, but still have doubts about their abilities and see their potential for errors built into their psyche. Their thoughts in close games are usually "...Please don't let them hit it to my son."

I can honestly say that not once this year did I ever say to myself, "I hope they don't hit it to him or him!" My firm belief is that each and every player is fundamentally sound. The trust I have in them can be felt by each player. Getting to this level in the tournament, I feel that we have evolved to the point that if our player can reach the ball, he will successfully field it. Each of our players has reached a level of accountability and takes full responsibility for the position he is playing.

An important aside is that at this tournament our laundry needs to be done by us; the American Legion and the hotel are not responsible for it. My wife Lynda and a couple of mothers take on this task with no complaints as though they accept it as their way to help and thus change from fans to an integral part of the team.

We draw the Michigan State Champion as our first opponent, a team from a small town of some 3,000 people coached by Larry

Tuttle, a man who knows not only how to teach the game, but a coach who is becoming a high school baseball legend. His team this year features a major league bound pitcher, strong hitting, and a terrific defense. I soon find out that he not only knows everything about his team but he also knows everything about the teams he's playing against. He knows about our pitchers, our all American shortstop and our power hitting third baseman.

This first game goes to eleven innings with each team having chances to win earlier but falling short. There is a game-changing play when Coach Tuttle holds up his runner at third because Bill Schell stopped the ball in short left field and he is sure that Schell can pick up the ball, whirl and throw his runner out. Were I in that position, I would have sent him and forced his shortstop to make that throw. He knew too much about Schell. Meanwhile, Jeff Coker crushes a ball towards Western Europe for his fourth homerun in as many tournaments and has the crowd in shock and awe every time he comes to the plate after that. The final score is 3-2, with Greg Heyde pitching all eleven innings.

The Kentucky State Champion is next. About three hours before the game, an issue arises that I don't anticipate. Dave Hankins had gone to Missouri to enroll in college and isn't back yet. I talk his father into going to O'Hare personally to pick him up and bring him back to the field. Luckily his flight arrives on time and we are ready to go at game time. I predict a one hitter but I really don't know if Dave is going to be ready so soon after his trip.

Hankins is masterful on the mound scattering three hits and not walking anybody. Our team had eight base runners with four hits and four walks. Throughout the game we keep pressure on them on the base path but the well-coached Kentucky team makes defensive play after defensive play throwing out runners. In the bottom of the sixth Shepherd drills a single to left. Heyde follows with a bunt that is misplayed; he gets to first as Shepherd moves to third. This is our chance to force the issue. I give Heyde the steal sign, and he moves to second safely. With men on second and third in scoring position, I can see that Kentucky is really nervous for the first time in the game. I call the suicide squeeze bunt and the Kentucky pitcher plays it correctly. He throws it high and outside and it takes all the reach that Jeff Kowatch has, but he makes contact and puts the ball in play scoring Shepherd from third. When the dust clears it's Post 50 one and Kentucky zero. That run is all Hankins needs, as he finishes the game shutting them out the rest of the way.

After this game, an announcement is made that a new record had been set by the Indiana Team. The most trips ever to a concession stand in a two game period, and it was set by number ½ , the bat boy, Todd Machuca, who always seems to be holding a candy bar, snow cone or bag of popcorn.

With the shutout against Morehead, KY, we stay in the winner's bracket and have gained the right to challenge the defending National Runner-up, Arlington Heights, Illinois. It's like jumping from the frying pan into the fire. After playing two very classy teams like Blissfield and Morehead we are now face-to-face with the most vocal and arguably the strongest team in the tournament, Arlington Heights, IL; they have just crushed the Ohio Champion 21-3. Like us, they have won their first two games. Whoever wins our game will be in the catbird seat, will have Saturday off and wait for whoever comes out of the loser's bracket. They will have to lose twice to be eliminated.

To this point in the tournament, Heyde has gone a full eleven innings against Michigan but because of a rain delay has his twelve innings of pitching eligibility. Hankins has thrown the full nine against Kentucky and has three left. I decide to go with Janiszewski against the Illinois State Champion, even though he had a tough time in our state finals. Jano is a finesse pitcher with a great curve ball and I have watched Arlington Heights destroy all the heaters they had thrown at them. In addition he is eighteen years old and one of our senior pitchers.

Arlington Heights lives up to their hype. They rock Jano for seven hits and five runs in the first four innings. Conventional coaching wisdom says when you're four runs behind you don't waste a pitcher you may need later in the loser's bracket. You should relieve with a pitcher you know you can waste. I can't do that! My mind is set on staying in the winner's bracket. We have to stop them from scoring. I know that if we can, we have enough time left to win this game. All of my thoughts are on this game. That's why you play nine innings.

When I make the pitching change I call on Greg Heyde to stop them. It brought up axiom #4 "Do it now!" Greg is in the zone. As he holds them to zero runs in each of the remaining innings, we come to life and start chipping away at their 5-1 lead. Each inning, I keep saying to the team …"Get me one run this inning and we'll win this game," and they deliver. We score one run in the fourth, the sixth, the seventh and tie it in the eighth at 5. After we get them out in the top of the ninth the stage is set.

Heyde leads off the inning with a walk and moves to second on a wild pitch. As I go through the signs, I can see out of the corner of my eye that Greg has an aggressive walking lead. Kowatch sends a sinking line drive towards right. As Greg takes off toward third, our eyes meet and we are immediately in sync …"Lets win this game on this play". The right fielder, who had thrown out, a very fast Dan Szajko at the plate earlier, fields it cleanly and sets to throw. My left arm is already in motion sending Heyde home and as his foot meets third base he uses it as a launching pad toward the plate. After passing third he sees that a good throw will nail him, so our 5'8" 160-pound iron man instantly decides he's going to take out of their 6'2" 210-pound catcher who is standing on the plate waiting for the ball. Greg lowers his head and squares his shoulders to set himself for the collision. On impact, their grunts can be heard across the field as Heyde is forced down onto the plate. Their catcher is knocked backward, loses his footing and goes down with Heyde. At the moment of contact, time seems to stop. An instant later the ball slowly rolls out of the catcher's mitt onto the grass. The umpire stretches his arms out, signaling safe. It seems like it takes several seconds for everything to set in but then our bench erupts realizing we have just defeated the Illinois State Champions.

Our team was almost magical in this comeback, we not only

out scored them but even with their overpowering start, we out hit them 12-11. Greg Heyde scattered four hits and kept them scoreless the rest of the way in relief of Jano. Meanwhile eight different players hit safely. Nine out of our ten players were on base. Not once in any inning did we go down 1-2-3. As a matter of fact we not only scored six runs but we left twelve on base. Talk about constant pressure. This is the zenith of our tournament play so far and the epitome of a team effort, against a team that was favored to walk through the tournament.

The Illinois Champion brought with them, either the final step in our metamorphosis or at least the venue for the manifestation of the changes in our decision making processes. Whichever it was, this game provided us with the chance to stand toe to toe with one of the strongest and physically largest teams in the tournament. We did that for a full nine innings and came out ahead.

It is in this game where we have an unfair advantage because our seventeen people took on their individual super stars one at a time, an inning at a time. It is also the game that everything I have been professing all season long comes to fruition.

Our team has been relentless throughout this tournament beginning with the sectional games in Indiana. We believe that everyone on the team can and will contribute and they do. Now we have only one team left to face but no matter who it is, we know that we have beaten them before.

After what seems like an eternity, because another rain delay has interrupted the tournament for two days, we are at last arriving at the Championship game. From our standpoint, the best part of this is that someone will have to beat us twice in order to eliminate us and move on to the American Legion World Series. We are waiting for either Blissfield or Arlington Heights. The worst part of it is that both teams believe that they can beat us. This may work to our advantage because while each is thinking about how easy it is going to be to defeat us that they aren't thinking about playing each other. Larry Tuttle, the Michigan coach, comes to his senses first. He knows that he has to beat Arlington Heights before he can even begin thinking about us. The Illinois team it seems is already planning a return to the National Finals.

For our part, psyching-out our opponents in advance is not even an option. We wait to see who it will be. We aren't in for any surprises but neither team will be a cakewalk. In this tournament, we have registered three consecutive one run victories. Our advantage is that most of our pitchers have their full complement of innings left with the exception of Heyde with 6 and Jano with 8, since both had thrown against Illinois. Either of the teams we will be facing would have used a minimum of five pitchers already and will need at least two more to accomplish the feat.

Blissfield survives a 10 inning 3-2 battle with Arlington Heights. So there we are facing a class team. The only thing we have to do now is to play the game. We are definitely prepared to do that. I again go with Hankins, since he usually follows Heyde and his confidence level is peeking after the 1-0 shutout game against Kentucky.

We have some changes we have to make on defense because Coker has an injured ankle. I move Shepherd to third from second, Andert to second from first and bring in Marc Toles to play first. We are as strong defensively as we were with our other lineup. I feel like we are set for Blissfield if Hankins can pitch his usual game.

As stated earlier, defense and pitching are synergistic. In the eleven inning game that follows, Blissfield is able to get 13 runners on base while we get 15. It is the defenses of each team that keep the game scoreless through 10 innings. The pressure is constant as each team threatens to break things open during the game. Good pitching and defense prevent that from happening twice for Blissfield and twice for Post 50. Finally, in the eleventh with no score, Heyde singles to open the inning but is forced at second on a grounder by Kowatch. Dan Szajko follows with a walk and Madey lays down a perfect bunt to move them to second and third. With first base open they intentionally walk Coker, who is pinch hitting; this loads the bases with two outs. This brings to the plate Dave Hankins who is an outstanding pitcher. Suffice it to say hitting is not his strong suit.

With the help of a couple of take signs Dave has worked the

pitcher to a full count and is confident that he can make contact. I give him another take sign and he asks me to repeat the sign, so I do. It is then that he calls time out and walks toward me at the third base coach's box. He says "Coach, do you know the count is full and you gave me a take sign?"

I reply, "Yes."

He asks, "Why?"

I respond calmly, "It's because I don't want you to swing at the ball."

He said, "Coach, I know I can hit it!"

I counter in a whisper, "Dave, if you swing at the ball I'll tear your arms out at the sockets!"

Dave understands and takes the pitch for ball four, forcing in Kowatch from third for the first run of the game. It goes down as an RBI, and as it turns out the winning run which makes Dave happy on both counts. Then Schell walks forcing in Szajko and Coker scores on an error on an Andert ground ball giving us a 3-0 lead.

Blissfield opens their eleventh with a walk and a hit, but Dave gets the next three on a strikeout, a pop out and a force out. The most closely contested tournament I have ever been involved in is over. We overpowered no one. We simply played consistent, controlled baseball. The entire team is focused and it appears that we have arrived. We are the Great Lakes Regional Champions!

The rain delays washed away any chance of our going home even for a change of clothes. Instead we are whisked away on the wings of United. Our next stop is Manchester, New Hampshire and the American Legion World Series.

BOTTOM OF THE 6TH

In almost all team championship journeys, there seems to be a defining segment, key time period, or critical moment that you can look back on and realize that it was here that the team became championship caliber. Records don't define them at this point, statistics are virtually meaningless, and where they hale from matters even less.

They evolve to a higher level of play. They create even more confidence. They elevate their collective game. And they mature.

For our baseball team that place and time was Bellwood, Illinois at the Great Lakes Regional. It was here that we became a legitimate force, not only for our opponents, but in our own psyches. We moved onto the national stage in Bellwood, with everyone sensing our competitive maturation.

Quite simply these were the best games, the toughest competition. We were out of our minds...

Game #1 – Blissfield, Michigan.

Jeff Coker Day. He hits another major bomb, off Ray Soff this time, a future major league pitcher with the St. Louis Cardinals, extremely close to the crowded community swimming pool in left-center. Probably injured in a bad way a couple of elementary kids. No big deal to Jeff, or us for that matter. I can hear the community pool director now on his microphone, "For the safety of your children ladies and gentlemen, I know it's hot and all, but please make sure they are not near the pool or playground area, and are tucked safely into our nuclear bomb shelter when the third baseman from South Bend is at bat. Thank you very much and enjoy the rest of your day". A bases loaded walk to Coker in the 11th wins it. They were very good. I guess we were too.

Game #2 – Morehead, Kentucky

Somehow I get to third later in the game, the 6th inning. 0-0 score. Both pitchers are dealing some good stuff at the other team. Mel calls for the squeeze play. Perfect. Kowatch will come through of course, of that I have NO doubt. Then I remember thinking that somehow I've got to get to home plate before they can make a play on me. I know what to do and what not to do. The big guy on the mound for them is in the stretch. I've seen him and can pretty much time it up. That is if I don't panic at the very last second and give it away, or he gives me an extra look before throwing. Bad news. Both kind of happened.

As soon as I broke I knew I blew it, but you have to keep going hoping for a wild pitch, or a hit by pitch (sorry Jeff, but I know you'd take one for the team or to save some serious embarrassment for your lifelong friend), or God to strike me dead with a lightning bolt for making such a stupid move in a BIG situation. Their pitcher makes a perfect pitch out to the right handed hitting Kowatch. Jeff, with only his left hand on the bat makes an unbelievable stab at the pitch, letting go of the bat, with his left leg lunging toward the first base line. Somehow, we still don't really know how, he makes perfect contact and the ball rolls innocently toward the first baseman and I scamper across the plate with what proved to be the winning and only run scored in the game. You couldn't have rolled it onto the field any better, let alone toss the bat and hit it while doing a dance. Nothing short of phenomenal effort and brains on Jeff's part.

The Kentucky players, coaches, and fans came out of their shorts screaming that Jeff had stepped on or over the plate when he made contact. The catcher who was standing upright ready to catch the ball and tag me out easily couldn't believe what he just saw. Neither could we. The good guys won that argument and the run stood. Woody Miller called it the "Lancer Special" in the newspaper. He also made reference to my mother attending Morehead State University in the article. We both got a little ink back home and she thought that was real special too. Hank put up zeroes the whole game. He never cracked. Neither did the defense. Life was good. So were Kowatch and Hankins.

Game #3 – Arlington Heights, Illinois (1976 National Runner-Up)

We tie it in the eighth on a hit by Schell, win it in the ninth on a hit by Kowatch. Jano and Heyde combine to keep us in the game. Jano got roughed up very early, and Greg came in and shut them down and out the rest of the way. Heyde just willed all of us to get it done. We rode him like a Derby favorite at Churchill Downs. Mel wasn't saving anyone. He knew we could win this game, and he also knew that we needed Greg to do his thing, and he did, again! He also scored the winning run in the bottom of the ninth on a collision play at the plate. He was dead to rights, but Mel sent him to make the right fielder make the perfect throw to keep us from winning. The place was rocking and rolling as he rounded third with everyone watching the throw. The outfielder threw a dart, on the money to the catcher. He and Greg got up close and personal, and the ball popped out of his mitt. Our dugout and the whole place, it seemed, exploded. Dynamite comes in small packages sometimes. Be careful if it says "#2 – South Bend, Indiana".

This was the most satisfying win of the tournament for us because these guys, their coaches and fans, were completely full of themselves. I guess they had a right to be because they were good, very good. But they were also big on running their mouths a lot. I hate that. We hate that. Maybe not all of them, but enough of them to make you bear down and make plays to beat them at all costs. We were down 5-0 very early, we win 6-5 in the bottom of the ninth. Another late inning comeback by the guys from Indiana. Never say never.

We had a lot of smallish quicker guys, not many guys over 6'0 tall, and no left-handed guys. Every team had bigger, stronger guys but the good thing about baseball is you don't have to have those kinds of bodies to win. We went to a White Sox game the next night. We'll let the loser's bracket play while we check out the pros at old Comiskey Park on the South Side. The break after these three games couldn't have come at a better time. We definitely earned the night off. No one who saw us play in Chicago would deny that. Life was good, and getting better.

Game #4 – Blissfield, Michigan

They climb through the loser's bracket and need to beat us twice to go to Manchester. We would just as soon get it over with and start the party, but a rain out in about mid-game sends it to the next day, plus we do another 11th inning number on these guys. Hank shuts them out, although I remember they seemed to have runners on base a lot in that game. Nervous Nellies need not apply. We score 3 in the 11th and we're off to New Hampshire. Literally we were. We went back to the hotel, showered quickly, headed to the airport, and were out of there.

We played tremendous one-run baseball in Chicago. Extremely pressure packed games and plays; real heads up, aggressive ball in all phases of the game. The best "crunch time" baseball I've ever been a part of at any level. We deserved to represent the Midwest region (Indiana, Illinois, Kentucky, Ohio, Wisconsin, and Michigan). We had defeated some outstanding teams and pitchers. I have a great picture that my sister, Andy, took of me through the fence in Bellwood after the final game, and the look says it all. I'm emotionally exhausted and it looks like the weight of the world just got lifted off of my shoulders.

My mother wanted a picture of me with the trophy after the championship game so I asked Mr. Kouts, our Post 50 Baseball Chairman, if my mom could get a shot of me with the trophy. He was carrying it out of the ballpark on his way to our bus. He smiled at me with his huge victory cigar sticking out of the side of his mouth. He says sure. I assumed he would let me handle the trophy by myself. I reached for the trophy and he turns to my mom and smiles for the camera, with the tightest death grip on that trophy in the history of American sport. No way was he letting some punk kid who needed a major hair cut handle this piece of hardware by himself.

This was Post 50's trophy which meant that for the time being it was HIS trophy. It was going to make it back to the Post in South Bend without a scratch or mark on it, let alone my sweaty palm prints. I'm barely in the picture. All you really see are his huge white knuckled hands on the big trophy, and the Boston Celtic victory stogie. You would have had to use a high caliber gun to pry that thing loose from him. It always brings a smile to my face every time I recall that moment, or see that picture.

The real trophy though, awaited one of eight National Regional Champions in Manchester, New Hampshire. We were on our way to see if we could get our sweaty palm prints on that one.

SHEPHERD #11
"To Mel and #2"

Game #3 – Arlington Heights, Illinois (1976 National Runner-Up to Santa Monica)

After two years of dissecting our season and looking at the details of how we did what we did and writing about it all, it has occurred to me that I took your performances (both Greg Heyde, player and Mel, coach) against Arlington Hts. much too lightly. We were in our deepest peril versus arguably the most talented team, and because of both of you we were able to pull it out of the fire.

Yes, the other one-run games and extra inning games in Chicago were "crunch time" victories in their own right against outstanding individual talent and teams, but it was the Arlington Heights game and the 9th-inning victory that solidified for sure that our incredible momentum would not be slowed down or stopped. Kentucky and Michigan were extremely talented teams, no question about it. Any baseball person with an ounce of sense could see that. But what I think everyone takes too lightly is the fact that Arlington Heights was National Runner-up the season before. They had been there, done that!

They had ten returning players from their second place finish the year before, solid players at all positions and no perceived weaknesses. They didn't quit when we started chipping away at them, we just overcame mainly because we didn't let them score anymore. To make the best and most important coaching decision of our tournament life...and to answer the bell and shut them out for the entire game after coming in, these were the best performances of the entire experience, at least in my humble opinion. It doesn't diminish in any way the outstanding individual performances we received from so many players throughout the tournament, but in my mind both of yours' ranks as #1. (I just wanted both of you to know how I feel about it...FOR THE RECORD. And at the next available opportunity I will drink a Maker's Mark and Coke in celebration of your outstanding performances and in your honor.)

" "

SHELL #3

Once we won the state, I was somewhat satisfied. I was just thinking the regional would be a good time away from home...how wrong I was. I think that is where we became "The Team". Everyone contributed. It was a total team effort.

ANDERT #7

I remember getting beaned by Ray Soff in the tournament. My elbow swelled up like a balloon, and then I think he promptly picked me off first base. I'd like to think I was just letting the rest of my teammates see what kind of move he had to first. I'm sure it paid dividends later in the game.

I remember Bill Schell's being constantly on second base ... even after he struck out or so it seemed.

COKER #19

There was no doubt in my mind that Mel was quite knowledgeable and well schooled in the fundamentals of baseball. But I do believe that his best attribute as a coach was his decision making during games. Quite often, these decisions were not always "by the book", but were gut feelings based on his knowledge of his players' unique strengths and weaknesses. To me, that sixth sense is what makes some coaches better than others.

MADEY #12

Hankins had a great two games with his best pitch which was a slider and given the fact that he could throw it where I asked for it, I called it often. His slider would start inside and bend to hit the inside corner or on the outside corner then move slightly out of reach of the hitter. This allowed him to throw a fastball occasionally which the hitter would take because he didn't want to look foolish swinging at a pitch he thought would be fading out of the strike zone.

Greg had an incredibly hard fast ball that would rise slightly and move left to right. His speed was rarely matched by any pitcher we saw and kept the joint on my left index finger bruised and swollen the entire summer. He also had a good fast curve and even tinkered with a knuckle ball. Imagine seeing a 90-mph fastball on one pitch and a knuckle ball on the next.

RUDASICS #8

While the day started out with our being backed to the wall, it may have been the greatest moment in sports history when we came back and beat Arlington Heights.

SZAJKO #4

"We had the trust and confidence in all of our teammates, that if a hit was needed, or a play needed to be made, or a certain pitch thrown; we knew that it was going to happen."

TOLES #9

I think Chicago helped us to get to know each other at a whole new level. Our play moved from methodical and precise to include rhythmic and fluid. A maturity had set in that was taking us a little beyond our years, both in terms of our play and confidence. We finally figured out what our coach had been telling us the whole season. It didn't matter if our opponent was better than we were; they still had to beat us on the field. We just didn't believe anyone could anymore.

Back Row: Dave Hankins, Jeff Coker, Jim Andert, Dave Yates, Mark Toles, Scott Madey, Dan Toles,
Middle Row: Bill Barcome, Dan Szajko, Bill Schell, Mike Clarke, Dom Romeo, Jeff Rudasics, Mel Machuca
Front Row: Dennis Janiszewski, Greg Heyde, Todd Machuca, Jeff Kowatch, Will Shepherd, John Ross
Missing: Bob Kouts, Gary Vargyas

Mr Kouts always has a grip on the situation

7TH INNING

American Legion World Series

"I searched for glory and glory I did not see.
I searched for victory and victory eluded me.
I searched for teamwork and found all three"

TOP OF THE 7ᵀᴴ

Upon arriving in Manchester, New Hampshire I realize that every aspect of our trip is as structured as the Chicago trip had been. Our flight is on a chartered plane. We have to get to Manchester on Tuesday for the banquet. The scheduled speakers are Bowie Kuhn, the commissioner of major league baseball and Tom Gorman, former National League Umpire. The legendary pitcher Bob Feller of the Cleveland Indians and former American Legion player, is a guest. It is evident that George Rulon, the National Baseball Director, who very much resembles General Patton, runs a great program and a very tight ship and doesn't leave any aspect of this tournament open to interpretation. He is clearly the "Commanding General". It is clearly his tournament and he is going to run it his way. A list of the rules is given to us in writing; he has been doing it for many years and each year the logistics became cleaner and smoother. It is also made clear that you are here only to participate in the tournament.

This is the fifth and final level of the tournament, the national finals or officially, The American Legion Baseball World Series, in which the eight National Regional winners compete. There is no automatic entry for a host team at this final level.

The rules, as they are written, are that when your team suffers two losses you are eliminated from tournament play. At that time your team will return to the hotel and be sent home as soon as humanly possible, sometimes within an hour after returning to the hotel. You can not stay there an extra day to watch the other teams play. He does not want the responsibility of having any idle teen-agers doing damage to the hotel, hurting themselves or marring the image of the American Legion Baseball World Series. These procedures are explained to all of the teams as part of a tournament orientation meeting. Mr. Rulon makes sure that all participants are as aware of these rules as they are of the baseball rules.

Each team is met by an assigned team host who is permanently attached to that team. Ours is a local and has been well versed in anticipating what our needs and or our wants might be. They move us around from the hotel, the stadium and the practice fields by bus and we are on a strict military time schedule. We move from airport to hotel registration to tournament sign-in to banquet sign-in. Each team has to do everything by the numbers. We take official pictures at an assigned time and we practice at an assigned time. You can't be late or the bus will leave without you; if you miss practice, you can't make it up.

Meanwhile, Woody Miller, our unassuming sports writer with the South Bend Tribune who has traveled with us throughout this tournament, is here again. Woody, is a realist; I need him nearby. He has become my barometer. He doesn't say much, I now under-stand his every look. His baseball knowledge was gained from all of his years as a sports writer. He is always ready to assess the talent of the teams we are playing, so much so, that I am sure that he is researching them through one or many of his newspaper contacts that he has built over the years. His ultimate act of interest and loyalty to me manifested itself when he volunteered to drive my wife and son to Manchester, New Hampshire so they could follow us to the World Series of American Legion Baseball.

He plays a very important albeit low key roll in our search for success when we are in New Hampshire. After scrupulously watching all the teams practice prior to our first game in the tournament, he comes to see me. In his inimitable manner, he looks me straight in the eye and says in very muffled but convincing tones, "I haven't seen any team here that you can't beat!" Let me make it perfectly clear what he did not say. He did not say that there was no team here that couldn't beat us! I heard him clearly and it was exactly what I needed to hear. With that statement alone, my confidence leapt. The realist himself stated it. No fluff, just one clear statement. Not who to pitch against whom, not who to play in the field and definitely not how to defense them or what to expect from them.

From my side, I'm not going to change my approach anyway. Someone is going to have to prove that they can beat us. We had just come through the toughest tournament in which I had ever participated, three one-run games, two won in the last inning and two 11-inning games. Talk about intensity. This team of eighteen year olds did it without showing any of the stress that many thought they surely may have felt. I chose not to over emphasize it. I decided to treat it as though it were business as usual. We can beat anyone we play as long as we keep it all in perspective. An inning at a time, I keep thinking it and repeating it over and over in my head. We now move to the final and highest level of this tournament.

No one that I know has ever reached this point. South Bend Post 284 finished fourth in the Nation some years before but I wasn't involved in American Legion Baseball when that happened. Even Bob Kouts, Post 50's baseball chairman who had been involved in American Legion Baseball for over thirty years, wasn't there. So no one could give us any insight as to what to expect. This is probably a blessing. We have to experience it for ourselves.

So here we are taking part in a tournament in a field of the eight best teams in the country. There is no host team at the National Finals. Each team in this field has earned its position by playing through their state tournaments and their National Regional Tournament. All of them are state champions. It was like making "who's who!" in the country in American Legion Baseball. Again we are the smallest team and although we have a great record, our opponents' records are even better. Among this field many had programs that had been here before. This is the first time for our program at Post 50 to be playing at this level. The names of the other teams are firmly entrenched in my memory. Boyertown, PA (45 -2), Santa Monica, CA (41 -3) the defending National Champion, West Palm Beach, FL (29-2) Lewiston, ID (63-16), just to name a few.

I decide to go with the same pitching rotation we used successfully at the Great Lakes Regional in Chicago. "If it ain't broke, don't fix it!" was the way I looked at coaching baseball. These are our most mature and experienced pitchers and somewhere in the back of my mind I kept hearing Casey Stengel's axiom - "When ya finally get to da big dance, ya gotta dance wit the guy what brung ya!"

Our first hurdle was Boyertown, PA. I watch them as they confidently take the field for their pre-game warm-up and there is no doubt about it, they belong here. They look like a fine-tuned machine as they work through their routine. This venue is just another port on their journey. It appears that they have planned their whole tournament. Their least concern is the South Bend Post 50 team. They seemingly see us only as their warm up to playing against the defending National Champion and getting on with their goal of winning this tournament. California has to be the odds on favorite to repeat, but not to Boyertown, they're here to win. Today they have to put us into the losers' bracket in order to get to Santa Monica.

On our side of the field, although Pennsylvania can't even imagine it, we are just as confident as they are. In my mind, none of the teams here can possibly surpass what we faced and defeated in Chicago. We take the field like we own it! We are ready to take on today's opponent and make them beat us. We aren't about to give quarter to anybody. They're going to have to prove that they can beat us, here on the field, not on paper, or in a straw poll. In sales there is a saying, don't tell me how good you are, put it on the sales sheet (PIOTSS). In baseball tournaments, the same is true, put it on the scoreboard.

Greg Heyde is our opening pitcher as he was throughout the tournaments we have already played to get here. His regular season and tournament record is 13 –1. Two of those wins were last week in the National Regional. The first against Blissfield, MI in an eleven-inning complete game and the second was against the defending National Runner Up Arlington Heights, IL in 6 innings of relief. I know that if he has to throw hard for twelve innings today, he could do it. He has a rubber arm and would throw every day if the rules would allow it. Furthermore everyone else on the team is healthy and ready. We were all in the Zone. No one said it, but we all knew it.

Against Boyertown, Schell and Coker go into their act knocking in two runs apiece. Schell goes 4 for 5 including a triple. On defense, three double plays help Greg Heyde stay out of trouble and give him his fourteenth win against only one loss. South Bend out hits Boyertown 11 to 6 and we defeat them 5-1.

Our next opponent brings us to the realization that we are definitely taking the hard road to wherever we're going. We have already played and beaten last year's Runner Up and now we have to take on the reigning National Champion, Santa Monica, CA, who earn this spot by beating a 32-7 Trumbull, Connecticut team 9-2. They look as big as their pre-tournament publicity.

I select Dave Hankins to throw against Cliff Wenzel for Santa Monica; they both have 14 and 1 records. Dave has 23 consecutive shutout innings coming into this game, but Santa Monica makes short work of that when they score a run in the first inning on a walk and two hits. With one out and men on first and third, we know that we have to call on our defense. This time it was Jeff Kowatch who comes up with a dazzling off the fence catch of a fly to right, and fires to first to double off their runner. This holds California to a single run in the first inning. After tying the score at one in the bottom of the first, we unload on them in the second inning, bat around and score five more. Hankins gets stingy the rest of the way and although he walks four, he only gives up two more hits the rest of the game. At one point, he retires 12 in a row and 18 of 19 overall. Schell, who is now firing on all cylinders, gets four hits in four at bats and a stolen base to give him a two-game total of 8 hits in 9 at bats. We keep constant pressure on them on offense with 16 base runners. We didn't let them breathe. The result was Post 50 downing Santa Monica 7 to1.

Our next game is against what may have been the physically largest team in the tournament, Hattiesburg, Mississippi. They have been pummeling people on their way here. By this time our reputation is that we are a running team. The Manchester newspaper sports writer comes down before this game and warns me that they have a catcher who has been drafted by the name of Gary Pickering. He is big, strong and has a canon to second base. Citing the fact that he has gunned down several runners who dared to challenge his arm, he asks, "You've been stealing bases in every game, are you going to change your running game against Pickering?"

I give him a one word response, "Absolutely!"

Dennis Janiszewski starts for us even though he had been rocked in his last two outings, one in the Indiana state finals and the other in the Chicago Regional. I have a feeling he's due. I need to have a curve ball pitcher against this team because they have been pounding all of the heaters they have seen. Jano does a masterful job after giving up one run on two hits in the first. He scatters five hits in the final eight innings and walks no one.

As for our running game, we steal four bases and it would have been six if their catcher, Gary Pickering weren't charged with a throwing error. Offensively, we again keep the pressure on with 10 base runners, Clarke gets three RBIs and Jano, gets two when he singles in the eighth inning.

The Manchester News sports writer again appears in our dugout after the game and says, "I thought you weren't going to run on Pickering."

"We didn't, we ran on their pitchers! Pickering's arm is just too strong!" I stated flatly. The final score - Indiana 8 and Mississippi 1 and with that we move to the championship game where once again, someone is going to have to beat us twice to take the championship. As I stated earlier we are in the "Zone".

This is it! This is the big one. After a long season of trial and error trying to find out who would help us the most in what positions, it came down to this. Everyone has a role and everyone knows what that role is. On our team, three different players pull themselves out of the lineup at some point during the tournament to make sure that they don't let the team down by being less than 100 % and not able to make the play. So often in sports you hear a player lauded for being courageous for playing hurt. I think the opposite, if a player is hurt in any way that makes him less than 100 %, he shouldn't be playing. I think taking yourself out of a big game demonstrates unselfishness, responsibility and accountability and an overwhelming respect for your teammates. So I am not concerned. I know everyone is healthy and ready for this game.

That's why you carry a full roster rather than just 9 players. If your backup players aren't good enough to come in and fill a needed gap, then they shouldn't be on the team. Too many coaches aren't willing or don't know how or when to use their backup players. Fortunately for us, ours are always ready to go when I ask them and today was no exception.

Throughout this tournament our pitchers have been extraordinary. In the past seven games I've only had to make one pitching change. For this game, **The Game**, I only have one pitcher on our staff who doesn't have 12 innings of eligibility left. That's Jano, who just gave me nine very strong innings. I have Yates and Hankins warming up in the bullpen the entire game, I don't want to play a second championship game.

Our opponent for **The Game** is again Hattiesburg Mississippi. This time they throw a 6 foot 5 inch big lumbering left hander with a mouth full of chew named Billy Wallace. He has a stinging fastball, a good changeup and a roundhouse curve that fools everybody. It seems like he steps halfway to the plate in his delivery. I of course choose to go with Greg Heyde. His five foot-eight-inch frame is poised to meet the challenge. As anyone can see, they are bigger and stronger than we are. So the advantage is ours! How's that for confidence? Besides we have our defensive team behind him, and by now we might be the best defense in the country.

In the second inning, Mike Clarke opens with a single and in our inimitable manner moves to second when Heyde beats out an infield hit. A bunt and a ground out is followed by a wild pitch that sends Clarke across the plate.

In the bottom of the second, Mississippi answers when Cavataio, doubles home Thornly, their right fielder, to tie the score at one.

In the top of the third, Schell leads off with a triple to the centerfield fence. With one out Coker walks and steals second. Shepherd then scorches the infield with a grounder that can't be handled by their third baseman scoring Schell and sending Coker to third. Now I need to keep the pressure on them. I give Shepherd a steal sign, something I hadn't done very often this year but now we're in the Championship game where you have to make things happen. In disbelief, he rotates his hands asking me to repeat the sign, I do sending Shepherd to second on the next pitch. When Pickering's throw hits the dirt in front of second and skips through to center, Coker virtually trots in to the plate for our second run of the inning. At the end of 2 ½ innings we're leading 3-1.

There is no scoring the rest of the way. Though this game will be remembered as a pitcher's dual and rightly so, I remember it as a defensive gem. Taking nothing away from Greg Heyde's performance on the mound, we had two monster defensive plays. One, a double play, started with a line drive to Shepherd at second after a twenty minute rain delay. The other was a Schell cutoff of a Kowatch throw from right field, following a single, relaying the ball to Andert at first to catch the runner who had rounded too far. It's like every player on our team is in perfect harmony.

Throughout the tournament this team has practiced what can only be described as controlled exuberance while still on the playing field. It is their trademark of winning with class. However, after the final out, the internal pressure has built up like a steam boiler and has to be expelled in some fashion and it is. The realization that the game has ended results in a moment of stunned silence. Then there is an explosion of jubilation, followed by a tidal wave of players running out to the pitcher's mound piling on top of one another. After order is restored by the American Legion officials, we regain our composure and are sent back to our dugout to wait until Hattiesburg is presented with their awards as the National Runner-up team.

The final test and the feelings it carried that happened with this team are analogous to what happened in the movie <u>The Natural</u>. The scene was early in the movie when Roy Hobbs struck out the "Whammer" on three straight pitches next to the railroad track with a small crowd watching. After the third pitch, Roy Hobbs, stood there, body still tense from pitching, snapped back closed fist and hit into his other hand in front of his chest as if to say, "There; I did it!" He knew it and no one could take it away from him. It was an inexplicable feeling of satisfaction.

Our feelings after the last game of the American Legion World Series are the same. No one has to say anything to anybody; we all have our own thoughts about what it means. "There; we did it!" and like Roy Hobbs, we mentally slam our fist into our other hand and know it.

Everyone is speechless; tears are beginning to well up in our eyes as the power of the moment is realized. Then it's our turn to receive our awards and as we move onto the field, I hesitate and watch them as they approach home plate with a combination of confidence and serenity. The once-in-a-lifetime dream game is over with a 3-1 score. The Indiana team, our team, South Bend Post 50, has won the American Legion Baseball National Championship. Now for the first time in two weeks, we can go home.

BOTTOM OF THE 7TH

College plans? What college plans? During the Great Lakes Regional in Chicago many plans for beginning the college school year were changed or cancelled, at least a few times for most of us. For some parents, players, and families, our tournament success was putting a real glitch into the best laid plans of mice and men. School or baseball? For some of us, we had a full plate to be sure. It was a real balancing act. Decisions needed to be made, details needed to be worked out, and we were doing that from a very long distance away from home.

Because of the many rain delays and postponements in Chicago, we were whisked off to New Hampshire on a plane very quickly after winning the Great Lakes Regional. For some of our team it was their first plane ride. Multi-tasking was for others with better organizational skills, like moms and middle-aged coaches. We were struggling just to get all of our stuff packed…again. We hadn't been down this road before. We had no real experience with this kind of travel for baseball; airports, itineraries, double check to remember your glove and spikes, etc. Where's my hat? Oh yeah, it's on my head…What a whirlwind.

Most of us were too jacked up to sleep much on the plane. I was lost in my own thoughts. I assumed my teammates were also. What were we heading into? We were clueless in every way. New Hampshire? We were aware of political primaries there, and people talking kind of funny, but the pinnacle of teenage summer baseball in New Hampshire? We would discover, along with all the teams at the World Series that at least Manchester, New Hampshire cares very much about baseball, and especially American Legion Baseball.

We had just successfully completed the most competitive tournament of our lives. Could the competition be any better than what we had just played through in Chicago? It was all the not knowing that made the anticipation so very strong for us. How would we be received by the fans? How many would there be at the games? What would the stadium be like? Would everyone's parents and families be able to make it? Our thoughts raced between things like, "So this is what the big time is like", to "I wonder if I have any clean clothes in case they have a banquet or some kind of ceremony"?

This plane trip to play the most important games of our baseball careers would also begin my almost schizophrenic behavior in giving up my luggage at airports that would last me a lifetime. I just know someone on the grounds crew or a luggage handler will five finger discount my glove or my bat. We'll get to New Hampshire without any equipment. I and my teammates would soon find out that our trust in the luggage employees at O'Hare International Airport was the least of our current concerns.

Airport Hanger – All the teams were to meet at the airport for instructions, rules, practice and game schedules, etc. I'll never forget sitting there in these folding chairs looking at the other teams who were already there, thinking that some of these dinky chairs are going to break in half, or these guys must have the wrong hanger and would someone please inform them the NFL Combine is on down a couple of buildings. Then we see some others come rolling in. The BIGGEST teenagers you could possibly imagine come walking into that room. I wanted to see some birth certificates and I wanted to see them right now, or I was going to represent all people 5'9" and under and weighing less than 185 pounds in a formal protest! Possible legal action if necessary! This looked liked a football callout meeting at Ohio State, not championship baseball.

I remember the "linebackers" from California being real loose. They had won it all the previous year, and came in looking like "O.K. which of these wanna be's are we going to put back on the plane first?" It had to be the largest contingent of really large baseball playing 18 year olds in America under one roof at one time. Florida, Mississippi, South Dakota, Idaho, Pennsylvania, Connecticut, California...What are they feeding these guys? And sign our whole team up for this nutritional plan.

GAME #1 – BOYERTOWN, PA

We opened the tournament against Boyertown, PA. They had and have great tradition in American Legion Baseball. Their record was off the charts. Only two losses and both of those had occurred during their tournament run. They were a clear favorite along with Santa Monica, CA. I remember this game as the Bill Schell Show. He went 4 for 5, scored runs, and stole bases and well, just about everything you would want your leadoff man to do in a big game to set the tempo for your team. We defeated them 5-1 as Greg Heyde pitched another outstanding game for us. Greg and Bill didn't wait for anybody else to get the word out that the Bad News Bears from South Bend, Indiana were here to win this tournament. Some of the press and people around us were a bit surprised at how well we played in all phases in that first game. We controlled it from start to finish. Aggressiveness and confidence were not in short supply for us at this point.

GAME #2 – SANTA MONICA, CA

The defending National Champions from California were our next challenge and they were loaded with big-time talent at every position. Everyone had heard and read about what an awesome team they had. For example, Tim Leary, a future UCLA Bruin, first round (2nd overall pick) draft choice, Major League pitcher for 10 seasons, and Big League pitching coach was their ace. I believe he won their first game against Connecticut. He helped the Los Angeles Dodgers win the 1988 World Series and pitched for seven Major League Teams during his career. And there were many others on their team headed to pro ball or Division I college baseball.

They began our game by jumping on Hank in the very first inning. It seemed like we had just started the game and before we knew it we looked around and they were all over us. Just as quickly though, their momentum would be squelched by my high school teammate in right field.

To this very day, one of the best, if not THE best, clutch outfield catches I have ever witnessed came when Jeff Kowatch jumped off one leg up against the wall at Gill Stadium in that first inning against Santa Monica to rob a guy of a sure double and possibly more. It stopped their early rally and they only posted a lone run for the entire game thanks in large part to his guts and athleticism.

We came back to tie that game in the bottom of the first when our outstanding shortstop Bill Schell (1977 American Legion Player of the Year) hit a leadoff triple and I got incredibly lucky and drove him in with a two out one handed swing that moved the ball out to left field in front of their outfielder. I was so badly fooled by their pitcher's curve ball that I took my top hand off the bat and tried to check my swing, and then realized that I might as well keep on swinging even with only one hand on the bat. I had committed too far already.

Every player from both teams, the umps, and the coaches knew that my quail into left was nothing more than dumb luck, and decent decision making. Their outstanding one loss pitcher, Cliff Wenzel, just scoffed at me from the mound when I reached first base. Smirked really, upon reflection, and that hurt my feelings too. Little did he know, or I for that matter, on the radio at that very moment, I was being heralded for my batters box discipline. The radio broadcast was pumped into both dugouts. Is that why all my guys are laughing themselves to death in our dugout when I peer in from first base? But my self-esteem survived the beach boy invasion that night.

On his first pitch to me I took a wicked hack (wicked for me that is) at a serious fastball and fouled it straight back. I had to be sitting fastball because he had thrown hard to every batter in front of me. I should amend that...VERY HARD it seemed to me, and I didn't want to be late on the one pitch that I could possibly handle, a straight ball. He came back on pitch number two with a nasty curve and I was fooled badly. Oh well, it looks like a line drive in the box score to those reading the morning paper in New Hampshire and South Bend. He was really * ^ # &! I tried to make it look as good as I could, standing on the bag like I did that everyday and twice on Sundays, but everyone in the park who knew anything about hitting knew it was complete * ^ # &!.

After our defensive inning, the guys in the dugout were really yucking it up because the play-by-play man on the New Hampshire radio station was saying that every youth baseball player in the country should take notes on how well I stayed balanced on the off-speed pitch and didn't over swing.

I deserved the crap I took, but the bottom line was getting that tying run on the board in the first inning gave everyone a little emotional lift, maybe Hank especially, because he knew that we were going to score some runs for him, and he didn't have to pitch a perfect game against the defending National Champions with the gaudy record, and all the USC and UCLA recruits and the draft choices. The real plays that inning were made by Kowatch, Schell, and Hankins. Some of my teammates had really good offensive games so we cruised to a 7-1 complete game victory on the back of Hank's pitching performance. Schell went 4-4, and Heyde and Clarke had big extra base hits for us that blew it open. Hank was in his groove from the start of the second inning to the last out.

GAME #3 – HATTIESBURG, MS

The excellent complete game Jano threw in our third game of the Legion World Series against Hattiesburg, Mississippi was just a classic in terms of guts and intelligence. They had an awesome offensive team, scoring tons of runs it seemed in their other games before they met us. To return from an injury, and to pitch like he did for nine complete innings against that lineup and give up only one run; well, it is just another example of how we had guys who stepped up when called upon. Always in command, and always pumping strikes with his off speed repertoire. He didn't give up a single walk. It was one of the gutsiest performances I have ever seen by a teenager on a baseball field in a pressure-packed game.

On that stage, after a couple of shaky appearances in the State Finals and Great Lakes Regional, against a team that had just been crushing the ball, we could not have dreamed up a better story or performance. Outstanding is the only word I can think of to describe what he did for our team that night. He had missed the entire regular season with his injury, so he was getting back into form on the run so to speak during the tournament.

His overhand curveball was devastating, one of the best I have ever seen, and he always made hitters think they could get it but he always had them out on their front foot too much, lunging for it. He sometimes would throw it every pitch for a whole inning, changing speeds and locations of course like all good pitchers. And it made his fast ball even sneakier. He took great pleasure in frustrating hitters and occasionally after a strikeout, that million dollar little *^#@! eating grin of his just cracked me up. He was careful not to show up opponents by letting them see it, but the guys who played on the infield with me got to see it a lot, and I think we all got a kick out of it, mainly because we did not have to embarrass ourselves by trying to hit the pitch ourselves. We won our third game in a row, 8-1, and again someone is going to have to beat us two games in a row to win this title.

GAME #4 – HATTIESBURG, MS

THE Championship game was against Mississippi again. This one is close though. I forget the score at this point in the game but it's tight. We eventually win 3-1. Bill is on third, Coker on second. I hit a hard bouncing grounder left of the third baseman, and he mishandles it, Bill scores, Coker moves up to third. The official scorer gives the rebel an error but I, my mother, sister, and brother believe it was an RBI base hit. I'm standing on first and Mel gives me the steal sign. He's obviously delusional at this point; or he, Beagle (coach Barcome) and the boys from the Post spent too much time in the hotel lounge last night, and it's affecting his judgment.

My name is Will. NOT Bill. And my last name is Shepherd. NOT Schell. I am <u>NOT</u> the William who runs the 6.65 60 yd. dash for the scouts. I'm thinking, no, I'm knowing that this is going to be ugly. I'll be thrown out by at least two full steps and the crowd will think our brilliant skipper isn't so brilliant anymore. I'm trying to think with my leader and I'm wondering why he didn't call for the hit and run instead? Why leave me out to dry in front of the

Yankee scout, who as we speak, is letting the ink dry on my free-agent contract? Mel, I don't want him to know I can't run!

The left-hander for Hattiesburg, who is headed to Mississippi State University when all this is over, has a real funky stretch and a great move to first. I decide in an instant that I'm going on first movement. At least it will look like an aggressive gesture on my part, and maybe the first baseman will throw the ball into left field and Coker can dance his way across the plate with a VERY important run for us. I break and as I near second I see the second baseman move to cover the bag in front of me. But in his eyes and face I sense worry and panic. The ball skips in front of the bag and short hops him, takes a wicked bounce into center field before their shortstop can back up the play and Coker scores easily. I use my technically sound pop up slide and for an instant think about trying to advance to third, but better judgment prevails and I decide that I better not push my luck. One base against this future Southeastern Conference Duo and I'll call it a career for stolen bases. Their catcher was drafted out of high school and he told me at the hotel he committed to play football and baseball for the University of Mississippi.

I'm not even sure to this day if I got credit for the SB or if they just gave the catcher a throwing error. That's not a knock at the catcher as much as it is a testament to my lack of true speed. As I'm standing on second I look over to my coach in the third base box and it all hit me in an instant. I get it now! You were pushing the right buttons again coach, putting the pressure on one of the best pitchers and catchers I had seen in my brief career, even if it was with one of the slowest hillbilly's you had ever seen in your long career. The point was, Coker was fast and had great instincts and timing. It could have been the Hulk on first and Mel would have given him the sign, just to give Jeff a chance to score. Brilliant! And I never forgot it.

That guy throws me out 99 times out of a hundred, but in that tense, pressure-packed environment, following the error, with so much riding on our momentum at that point, you put it in his lap to make the play, and the second baseman to make the throw to home, and he flinched, like you were counting on. Taking advantage of the situation. Our coach, and our players were real good at it.

FINAL OUT – OH NO!!!!! ANYONE BUT ME!!!! I JUST WANT TO WATCH THE FINAL OUT, NOT BE THE MAJOR PARTICIPANT. I WANT TO PARTY!!!!!

Two outs. One more to go to win it all. This championship counts for something. Over 3,800 teams from all over America started this double-elimination tournament in early August. The only time <u>EVER</u> on any baseball field anywhere, I ever say to myself, "Please, Greg, make them hit it to anyone but me. I'm done. I just want to watch, start partying, and sign my contract. Hey, where is my agent anyway? And while we're on it, WHO is my agent by the way? And where do I sign?" Of course, in the very next instant, and it was truly an instant, because the Baseball God is a fair and just God, and only allows players to be courageous ALL THE TIME, ground ball to my right. I choke it down, move over, field it, make the throw to Dert, and we all lose it for a little while. I wish all young people, not just athletes, could experience that feeling at least one time in their lives. Bedlam. True Chaos in Mudville!

Jano is the one kneeling beside me in the front row in all the different championship team pictures after we won at Gill Stadium in New Hampshire. In front of him and me in the picture are the spoils of victory; banners, trophies, plaques, etc. But the real spoil for me, the real pleasure for me, is to always enjoy the expression on some of the faces of my teammates, and Jano's especially, because it truly sums it up the best, at the time of the photograph that was taken and shown in the November, 1977 issue of <u>The American Legion Magazine</u>.

The Mississippi Runner-up Trophy and Banner had just been presented to their team and coaches, in pretty close proximity to us. Most of the press had turned their attention to that ceremony and presentation, but because of the many people and press still taking photographs of us, you get the truest, most honest reaction from a few of our guys. Coker and Jano are the best. Not everyone is looking at the other team, but these two are for sure. Their eyes say it all. The looks on their faces and the way they are looking at the southern boys who are singing Dixie and whooping it up, completely convince me that I was on the most perfect team for me to ever be a part of.

My most treasured picture in my baseball collection is the framed Championship Team Photo taken after the final out and trophy presentations. For that one brief moment in time, 1977, we represented the best 16 – 18 year old baseball team in America. We earned it on the field. All your team had to do was beat us to prove they could. No one did. This too sounded as good as it felt, "National Champions"!

❝❞

ANDERT #7
There was a successful balance of leadership, both leaders with pure baseball talent as well as those with the skill to keep the team loose and focused at the same time.

HANKINS #1
The truth of the matter is that we won games together and lost games together. Ultimately the same holds true for the National Championship. We won it together as a team. The pileup on the mound after the Hattiesburg game is in many ways symbolic of our team unity. We definitely have a bond that is unique and special.

CLARKE #5
"No play changed all of our lives more than the last pitch and the last catch in the last game."

SCHELL #3
We had a certain "grit" as a team and I think a lot of that was because of our small size. At the Nationals I remember getting our

pictures taken with the other teams and looking at how big they were and we looked like the Bad News Bears, but when it got to game time, the "Grit" always came out and we won.

JEFF COKER #19

I recall some trepidation that was inches away from doubt about our next opponent Santa Monica. First inning Hank on the mound, I remember the first three batters singling. They had runners on first and third one run already in and no one out. I recall saying to myself, "We got problems!" For the first time in the tournament I felt that we could be in for a long night. As quickly as that arose, it vanished when the cleanup hitter popped up for the first out. The next hitter hits a bomb to deep right where the always dependable Jeff Kowatch makes an unbelievable catch while running into the fence. Jeff had the baseball instinct after the catch to turn and fire the ball into first base to complete the double play. My thoughts from "We're in trouble", seconds ago, turned into "They're in trouble" as I mentally did a 180-degree turn while running into the dugout after "The Play".

ROMEO #13

"My biggest memory isn't a play. It was seeing every pitch from the vantage point I had watching you all win."

MARC TOLES #9

Sadly, Manchester is even more of a blur for me than Chicago. I had somehow misplaced the memory of Jeff Kowatch's catch in right field until someone started writing about it. Then it all came back, along with so many of the other plays and moments from that week.

I remember walking from the bus into the stadium for the first time. I have no doubt that we were ready for anything any opponent would throw at us. What we weren't ready for were little kids running up to us and asking us for our autographs.

I remember first stepping onto the field and thinking, we're playing in a stadium! It seemed so big, and I could just picture the stands actually being full, everyone watching *us* play; people rooting for this team from South Bend who didn't even know who we were.

But mostly, I remember watching the last man come to bat and thinking this is really going to happen. We are going to go 18-0 and win this whole damn tournament. And a few pitches later I was scrumming around on the infield with 20 of the greatest guys I will ever know.

SZAJKO #4
Overlooked, underestimated, underdogs, or overachievers; label us any way you like. We played and won as a team on the field against all of our opponents. The one thing that you should call us is winners.

DUGOUT CHAMPIONSHIP GAME
Coach and Batboy
Bill Barcome, John Ross, Dave Yates, Jeff Rudasics, Scott Madey

STANDS – GILL STADIUM – MANCHESTER, NH

POST 50 NATIONAL CHAMPIONSHIP
Gill Stadium - Manchester, NH

8ᵀᴴ INNING

Rewards

"Unexpected Benefits"

TOP OF THE 8ᵀᴴ

Early on the day after Labor Day, the day after the tournament, we're on a flight home to South Bend. As we taxi to the gate and approach the terminal we can see a crowd is there waiting for us. My wife Lynda and son Todd have flown home with us. It was a good decision because I wouldn't have wanted either of them to miss this. The Mayor, members of the city council, members of Post 50, family and friends are all there to greet us. We are presented with a Key to the City, followed by speeches and a parade.

The players have the trophies and National Champion banner. My job is to make sure we have everything. I hurry to the baggage claim area and as I am waiting for the luggage and equipment, the parade leaves without us. My wife, my son and I all miss it, but no matter, we are home now and we had won.

In the American Legion every team except the National Champion ends the season losing because it's a double elimination tournament with only one winner. This year is different for our team but only for us. We have put together a 25-game winning streak. The year is finally over and for the first time in my Legion coaching career, I finished a season on a winning note. I want to repeat this now, you don't win National Championships, they happen to you.

It was accomplishing our goal of winning the State Championship that gave our team the opportunity to participate in the National Tournament. What I discovered having experienced this tournament is that eighteen-year-olds are eighteen-year-olds are eighteen-years-olds no matter where they play. I also learned that the players in the warmer parts of the country do not have an advantage by being able to play the year around. As a matter of fact, most of them don't play one sport year around. They are just like the northern athletes.

The most important things I learned from this experience didn't even occur to me until after the tournament was over. This experience will give me an opportunity to try things about managing, leading and motivating people that I had only read about in business books or heard about in seminars I had attended. I am now convinced that anyone who is thinking about becoming a manager should have to coach in a youth sports program. The reason is simple, you have to teach, manage, motivate and direct, but you can't play.

Telegrams, cards and letters, begin pouring in from everywhere. Our governor, our Senators and Representatives, our mayor send us their congratulations. Baseball coaches from all over the state send mail, some I had played for, some I had coached against and some I had played against when I was younger but many are from coaches who had coached this team's players at one time or another. Their high school coaches are particularly proud of the players who had played on their teams.

The most heartfelt of these are hand written notes from former players and the families of these players and other players who had previously played for me. Other American Legionnaires send cards and letters and invite us to visit and schedule games with their teams in the future.

Local high schools have assemblies to honor the players. Those who are still in town feel the celebrity. I am interviewed on the radio, then on TV and then an in-depth one for the South Bend Tribune. These express the city's pride in our achievement.

The next thing that happens is that I receive a call from Tony Lucadello, a Hall of Fame major league scout, that the Phillies want to sign Jeff Coker right away. Dave Coker, Jeff 's dad, Len Buczowski, his high school coach, and I accompany Jeff to meet with Carl Lowenstein and Mr. Lucadello. It is a great moment for the Coker family.

Even with all of this happening something is missing. For the past twelve weeks we have been together planning for the next practice or game and suddenly it all ends; albeit a great ending, but it's an ending none the less. Suddenly, without warning, our lives change, because the tournament is over. The people we have been seeing everyday for the past five weeks, the group that we have been playing with, eating with and working with so closely on a common goal, scatter. Some go home back to their high schools, others are off to college and the rest go back to their real lives. The change makes one's arms feel like they are pulling on a string no longer attached to anything.

This should be the time for talking about how we met the dragons and slew them one at a time. We should be able to tell about how the little guys defeated the big guys over and over again. In each tournament we were the underdog, the unknown, the team that came out of nowhere. We were the smallest, the weakest, the slowest and the one with the least notoriety, and yet we were able to overcome all of the odds. Even if seeding were done in this tournament which it wasn't, the outcome would have been the same for us. In each tournament we beat the number two team twice. We defeated the defending National Champion and the defending National Runner-up. We defeated a team with a 45 - 2 record and another with a 41-3 record at the World Series level of the tournament. These are the kinds of games of which legends are made.

Instead what occurs is that we are no longer together as a team. There are only six team members who stay in town and they are in three different high schools. Another signs a contract and leaves to play professionally and ten scatter to colleges across the country. The players who stay home are in the best position to extend the celebration but subdue their feelings because they know that awards will be coming later when we're together again. I really don't know if any psychological harm will result from this, but it seams that I, their coach, am remiss in not conducting at least a debriefing following this much success and excitement.

After a couple of weeks I am able to inform them that one of the awards is that we will be attending the Major League World Series as guests of Major League Baseball's Commissioner Bowie Kuhn and of the American Legion. This will include being introduced on the field in a pre-game ceremony. I 'm told that we will be traveling to either New York City or Los Angeles, final plans aren't set yet, but we would be in one place or the other. Two days later, it turns out to be New York City.

No one on the team has ever been to a World Series game much less introduced on the field. I'm officially directed to notify the players that they will be receiving notification to plan to attend two games in New York City. The American Legion will pay for everything, airfare, transportation to and from the airport, from wherever they are currently located and also for our stay at the Statler-Hilton Hotel which is across the street from Madison Square Garden.

I couldn't have imagined a better or should I say bigger than life prize. We are actually guests of Major League Baseball; pinch me to make sure that I'm awake. We are taken to dinner at Henry's in the Bronx; following is a trip to the first game at Yankee Stadium. On the night of the second game, our host is Hall of Famer Monte Irvin who takes us through the Yankee clubhouse and through the tunnel past the Yankee dugout to the field. On our way the Yankees are coming off the field after their pre-game warm up. Most of them just pass us and we respectfully get out of their way but we are just excited to be this close to them. The last player off the field was Reggie Jackson, Mr. October, and we certainly don't want to get in his way. Suddenly he stops right next to me and asks, "Who are you?"

I smile and proudly state, "These are the American Legion Baseball National Champions from South Bend, Indiana."

Then Reggie Jackson does something that makes a lasting impression on all of us. Without hesitation, he turns and shakes the hands of all of our players and coaches and says …"I know what that means, I played American Legion ball too!" He is the only Yankee to do this at this point. Right after this we are introduced on the field to some 69,000 World Series fans.

After some pictures, following our introduction on the field, we are led off the field back through the Yankee dugout. As the Yankees begin returning to the field we again pause as they are passing us in the hallway and more of the players come over to shake hands with our team.

We are then escorted to our seats, my wife Lynda is already there sitting on the end of the row taking it all in. If you're familiar with Yankee stadium there are two and only two poles in the outfield. These are the foul poles in left field and right field, needless to say I sit immediately behind the left field foul pole and subsequently miss some of the game. Lynda is in the next seat over and can see the entire field.

After all of this it is hard to get back to what is happening in the state of Indiana. Following our National Championship accomplishment, I begin thinking that it would be important to have a voice in the state baseball program. I know it'll take a great deal of politicking which means that I'll have to go to the state American Legion meetings which are conducted quarterly in Indianapolis. I want to get Bob Kouts named to the state baseball committee. He deserves it. This will give us a voice in tournament locations and any rule changes that might come up. This unfortunately doesn't happen overnight. We talk about it but have to table it and place it in our ongoing project file.

Meanwhile, we still have to plan for a banquet. What kind of an award do you give to a team that has just accomplished the impossible? Suggestions start coming in from a lot of different directions. A local business man, Bill Screes, who has made collages for Notre

Dame national champion teams offers to make one for our team at his cost. It will measure 36 by 24 inches and each player will have one. The American Legion is going to give each player, coach and Post 50 a commemorative bat from Louisville Slugger. Baseball gloves, jackets and spikes are also thought about, but hands down, the players vote for rings. I couldn't agree more.

December finally arrives and the banquet we talked about right after the season ended is imminent. Players are returning from school. The National, State and local American Legion Officials have been invited to attend. Although I had anticipated having the banquet at Post 50, I was talked into having it at the Century Center, a newly constructed conference center in the middle of South Bend's business district. The Post 50 hall wouldn't have been able to accommodate the number of people we had coming. In retrospect the conference center's newness and décor actually added to the importance of the event.

A South Bend radio celebrity is our Master-of-Ceremonies and he really adds a professional touch to the program. In addition to the friends and families of our players, many of the coaches for whom these players had played at the younger levels are there. A special invitation was sent to their high school coaches since they deserved most of the credit for the baseball knowledge and skills these players had developed. Among the dignitaries present are Woody Miller of the Tribune sports department, the Mayor, the American Legion officers local, district and department level and, of course, George Rulon, National Chairman of American Legion Baseball whose tournament we had just won.

The keynote speaker, Tom Gorman, a former Major League umpire keeps the audience laughing which sets a positive but light tone for my introduction of the players and the presentation of the National Championship Rings. They have already received their commemorative baseball bat; it's black with all of their names embossed in gold, The collage of the team with individual team member's pictures has also been awarded. After I officially introduce them, I call them up one at a time to personalize the presentation of the ring that they have earned from Post 50 for winning this tournament.

Post 50 paid for these, but their value to the players and the Post far exceed any price tag they may have. As I call them up one at a time, Bill Barcome, my assistant coach, hands me the proper ring for each player presentation. You could actually see the pride in their faces as they walked toward the rostrum with backs straight, heads held high and their chests expanded.

When Bill and I finish with our presentation, a couple of the players, Marc Toles and John Ross, come up to me and in a whisper ask, "Aren't you going to give out the other awards?" The awards they are referring to are those that I present to the team in the name of never taking ourselves too seriously and emphasize the need to keep fun in this game. I have them ready so I agree to do it.

Again I call them up individually to the rostrum to receive an "ATTABOY" which is recognition for making something good happen in a game or something special about them. After they receive them, as they are returning to their seats, I immediately follow with an "OSHYTT" which makes them aware that dumb moves on the field or something about themselves is also noteworthy.

The templates for these awards, which took about 10 minutes to create, are hand printed with magic marker on white paper and ready to present. I hesitated presenting these in front of the dignitaries, mostly because I didn't want to embarrass anyone on our team. Presenting them turns out to be the right decision. The result is that the audience has as much fun as the players especially when they hear some of the categories; best looking, best hair-do, ugliest, getting picked off first, blowing a double play, among others. Yes we do have MVP and Best Attitude but those are serious awards voted on by the players. The coaches vote on Most Improved another serious award, but for the rest I take full responsibility. The next day the newspaper article just refers to them as the "silly" awards.

This baseball season was a journey that began on the Sunday of Memorial Day weekend in May and ended with a banquet on

Thursday December 22. It introduced us to many new people and opportunities that we couldn't have imagined before this very special season. So many of the things that will live in our memories we wouldn't have known were it not for this tournament. This experience brought us closer together than any group I had ever coached before or since. The most important part isn't the accomplishment as much as it is the bonding that takes place. We got to know each other, depend on each other, and trust each other. The tournament was merely the vehicle.

I believe that in asking me to present the fun awards, they were really saying, "Yes, we won the National Championship but that doesn't change who we are!"

BOTTOM OF THE 8TH

We vanished into thin air; baseball player one minute, professional student the next. Upon touching down in South Bend after staying the night in Boston, the day after our championship victory, Jeff Kowatch and I hurried off to our high school for a school-wide celebration in our honor. Jeff and I would gladly get our younger ex-teammates and friends out of class for a while, no problem.

We all had a plan, well, some general idea maybe that we should actually show up and start college in earnest. We needed a light switch and didn't have one. To go from the five-week roller coaster ride we had just enjoyed in American Legion Baseball to freshmen college student in about a 24 hour period was, to say the least, a little wild. Anxiety doesn't come close to defining what some of us were feeling as we tried to get organized for school again.

We would assemble our team again in October, in New York City for the Major League Baseball World Series. Mel called each of us to explain the details of our trip and give us instructions on the flights we would all catch to meet up in the Big Apple. THE World Series, not teenagers and amateurs, but men, professionals who play our game for a living. The best baseball players in the world, the Dodgers and Yankees getting it on for real. All eyes of the entire baseball loving world would be riveted on New York City and Yankee Stadium for the first two games. And we would be there in person, checking it out.

Dr. Yates, my Botany Professor at Butler University, during my first semester there said he was going to give me an F for the huge test I was going to miss because of the World Series trip. I remember standing before him after class one day trying desperately to explain the importance and magnitude of this trip. It was in front of some other students as well who were milling around. I was asking him if I could take the test early, or make it up upon my return. Reasonable requests I remember thinking. We definitely were having a major communication problem. Major difference in priority list here. I could sense some real trouble brewing.

In the back of my mind, through it all, I kept running through the many scenarios of how I was going to explain to my mother, through the bars of the Marion County Jail cell where I was now residing, after the finger printing thing and mug shots of course, that I was more than likely at least going to fail a 5 hr. lab class, be put on academic probation because of my low G.P.A., and lose the baseball scholarship that was one of my life-long goals. All because I had lost it and caved in this guy's face with my right hand that used to throw baseballs pretty accurately.

The red head from Magoffin County, Kentucky would not have handled that situation as well as some other mothers, maybe. I think not. I recall wondering if in the history of American incarceration was there ever a case where the mother of a college baseball player squeezed through the bars of a jail cell to get at her youngest son and beat him to death with her bare hands? All this in front of a couple of deputies with guns who don't know if they should ask this nice lady to join the force with them or draw their weapons on her.

I snapped out of my nightmare for a moment... Was this guy serious? **THE WORLD SERIES DR. SUESS**, I mean Dr. Yates. **THE CHAMPIONSHIP OF ALL CHAMPIONSHIPS! NEW**

YORK FOR THE FALL CLASSIC! Let's see now...Botany or baseball in the Bronx? You have got to be kidding me! Is this real? You know, Sinatra, "Start spreading the news". My teammates and I loose in the Big Apple. Perfect situation for a guy like me, in great need of another serious road trip, after a couple of months of academia at the "Harvard of the Midwest", beautiful Butler University.

To his credit, and maybe a little to my meaningless promise to make a better effort in his class in the future, he finally relented and we worked something out. I received a C in the class in December. Deserved it. Had the time of my life with my team in New York at the World Series in October. Earned that too.

We were the guests of Major League Baseball and the New York Yankees for the first two games of the 1977 World Series and were introduced on the field before Game #2 by Hall of Famer Monte Irvin. Over 69,000 people were in Yankee Stadium that night. Before the game we got a tour of the Stadium and the Yankee locker room by a member of the Yankee front office. We walked down the runway from the locker room to the field, through the Yankee Dugout, just like Ruth, Mantle, Mattingly, etc. We stayed in a plush hotel across from Madison Square Garden. It was outstanding in every way, and beat the hell out of going to class at Butler University and performing freshman pledge duties in my fraternity. All the east coast guys, and there were a lot of them in my house at Butler, wanted to kill the freshman puke for his tickets to the World Series. How Mel and the American Legion National Headquarters people in Indianapolis coordinated all of the different flights into New York I'll never know. We had guys in Missouri, Texas, and all over Indiana at that time going to school.

That trip started my allegiance to the New York Yankees. I've been a die hard fan ever since. I was a Reds fan until that trip. We got to meet some of the Dodger and Yankee players and I was just in awe of how large they all were, even the infielders, like Bucky Dent of the Yankees. Television does not really convey how big major league players truly are. Some guys were just flat huge. Steve Yeager of the Dodgers and Chris Chambliss of the Yankees looked like NFL defensive linemen to me. They all were so wide and thick. Watching those guys take BP was wild. People, including us, down the right field line where our seats were for the first game, were ducking and diving out of the way of some serious line drives that the awesome Yankee left-handed lineup produced…Jackson, Chambliss, Nettles, etc. If those balls happen to hit you in the head, you were dead. End of story.

Most of the players were real friendly and came over to shake our hands and talk with us a little. For example, Catfish Hunter, the starter for game #2, shook everyone's hand on his way to the bullpen to warm up. As he was about to get close to where I was standing he looked at all of us and said, "I don't know why I'm shaking all of your hands here tonight, you'll probably be taking my job away from me in a few years". Yeah, right. The Dodgers roughed him up that night and we had the perfect seats to watch the mayhem, left field home run seats about 10-12 rows up. When Dodger third baseman Ron Cey smashed an offering we all stood up immediately and panicked. It looked at first like it was going to land in our laps. It was close but over about 10 people so we had no real shot at it.

I regret not snaking a ball for all those guys to sign that night. A great opportunity lost because I couldn't breathe or move. Anyone who says they wouldn't be nervous in that kind of situation as a baseball playing teenager is flat out lying. That group of players and front office personnel from the '77 World Series was the subject of an ESPN Movie called "The Bronx is Burning" last winter. And yes, I watched every second of it, hoping to catch a glimpse of us on the field before game #2. It brought back some tremendous memories for all of us. Having conversations on the field with the best in the game, shaking hands with Hall of Famers, checking the Yankee locker room out before the game, those are memories that hopefully we can cherish for a long time.

We all have a great picture of our team holding our championship banner in Yankee Stadium getting introduced. The façade around the top of the Stadium is in the background. The stuff dreams are made of…

In December we all gathered at the Century Center in South Bend for our Awards Banquet. For those of us in college we had spent a couple of weeks enjoying our mothers' home cooking and seeing old friends. Now it was time to get together with the Post 50 gang and really celebrate our accomplishment. It was a pretty big deal. Local politicians, our high school Principals and Baseball Coaches, and the State and National Chairmen of American Legion Baseball were all on hand to offer us their congratulations and some really neat parting gifts for our personal trophy cases. Retired Major League Umpire Tom Gorman was the Guest Speaker and had everyone enjoying the evening with his funny stories from his many years in the Big Leagues.

The three most impressive gifts given to each of us that night were our rings, a black commemorative bat from Louisville Slugger with all of our names on it, and a picture and story collage of our remarkable season together. The most heart-felt gifts though were Mel's annual "Oh Shit" (he spells it differently on the actual certificate) and "At-A-Boy" certificates awarded to every player for various deeds from throughout the season. All of our team trophies, plaques, and banners were on display at a long table near the podium and until that night, I don't think any player had ever really noticed the hardware before. It was quite impressive.

Many of us still have our program from that Awards Banquet. The "Letter To The Graduates" written by Mel is the highlight of that booklet. It was the one detail that I will always remember about that night. I read it at my table and then looked around the room at all of my teammates and realized for the first time that this was a real honest to goodness "leave taking". The next phase of our lives had already begun and this night was the last time we would be together with this whole group of players, families, and friends. We each would go our separate ways after that night and there was no way to really sugar-coat it. Most of us would fade from the local spot light after this banquet; our futures were in other places, cities, and states for some of us. It was a perfect culmination and represented a lot of hard work and planning by our coaching staff and the folks from Post 50. It was first class all the way, and now that we're older we can really appreciate what everyone did for us that night. When you're part of the reason for one of these gala events and you're still a teenager, you just don't get it at that time. But you will.

Mens Restroom: Panama City Junior College Panama City, Florida Spring Break Baseball Trip – Frosh. Year - 1978

I'm standing at the urinal and I've got my Post 50 windbreaker on with all the patches, etc. It was an 8:00 A.M. game with East Tennessee State and it was breezy and chilly. This big guy from the other team comes in and starts to use the urinal beside me. He asks if I'm from South Bend and I say yes (I was born there, but lived about 16 miles south of town). He asks me if I played in Manchester last fall, and I say yes again, and he says that he pitched for the Rapid City, South Dakota team, and that he never in all his life saw a bunch of midgets who could play the game like we could. My reply, as I looked up at this lumber jack, was something to the effect of I had never seen so many big guys in baseball uniforms in all my life as I saw that week in New Hampshire. He smiled down at me and said, "Yeah, but it doesn't really matter does it? You won." I smiled and said yeah and thought...to the victor go the spoils, or something like that. Life was good.

COKER #19

The feeling of elation with disappointment. It was on a bus leaving Gill Stadium in Manchester, New Hampshire after defeating Mississippi 3-1. That game concluded our season with an 18-0 tournament record to give us the American Legion Baseball National Championship title. As elated as I was in that moment, I was also disappointed knowing that our team would never compete together again.

YATES #10

The whole tournament experience is one that will never be forgotten. It marked so many firsts in my baseball endeavors such as flying on a plane for the first time, being away from home for an extended period of time, being asked for an autograph, eating shark at a New York restaurant, standing at home plate in Yankee Stadium, getting Bob Feller's autograph, being part of a team that reached its pinnacle , receiving meal money, being followed by a homeless guy with a big gash in his forehead on the streets of New York City, having money sent to me via Western Union. These are all things that still mean a great deal to me.

Someone we can't forget in all of this is Todd Machuca who had the chance to ride along with his Dad. What a great memory for Todd and Mel.

ANDERT #7

In New York City, I remember sneaking out sometime after midnight with Romeo and Szajko and getting chased by a homeless man into an all night deli. The larger than life deli owner proceeded to come out from behind the counter with a baseball bat that may have been used by Paul Bunyan it was so big. He slammed it on the counter and threatened serious bodily harm to the bum if he did not hit the bricks, all the while asking if we wanted rye or whole wheat. What I really needed at that point was a new pair of boxers.

TOLES #9

I can still see six guys watching a girl dance on a table in a "nightclub" in New York City and the bouncer being kind enough to let a bunch of Hoosier hillbillies gawk for a while before asking us if we were going to stay or move on.

AWARD PRESENTATION
George Rulon – National American Legion Baseball Director
Mel Machuca – Manager of theYear
Bill Barcome – Coach of the Year

1977 TROPHIES
Scott Madey, Mark Toles, John Ross, Dave Yates – all returning

135

PRESENTATION FROM THE SOUTH BEND CITY COUNCIL

YANKEE STADIUM – 1977 WORLD SERIES
Post 50 Team Introduction
Hall of Famer – Monte Irvin

9TH INNING

Conclusion

*"It wasn't perfection, but it was excellence.
Excellence we achieved.
Perfection is God's business."*

M. Toles #9

TOP OF THE 9TH

So we did it. We had a team that had fun in its pursuit of excellence. We saw a window of opportunity open and we took advantage of it. This team literally "...filled the unforgiving minute with sixty seconds worth of distance run." We attacked it with all of the power of our being, defied the odds and were able to accomplish the "once in a lifetime" feat.

As hoped, our big guys performed beyond expectations on this National stage. Bill Schell won the Hillerich and Bradsby Batting award for highest batting average and was also named Player of the Year for American Legion Baseball. Jeff Coker was signed to a contract after the tournament ended with the Philadelphia Phillies organization for his outstanding play in high school and the American Legion Baseball Tournament. However, two players don't win a tournament like this by themselves. What happened with the other fourteen players is why we were able to complete an 18-0 run.

If there were a most valuable player award, we probably would have had sixteen or seventeen players to choose from depending on the game and the part of the season. It seemed that a different player rose to the occasion in each game. It happened on the mound and in the field. It happened at bat and on the base path. Sometimes it happened in the dugout or by someone taking themselves out of a game.

In a season where you can compile a record of 41 wins against only 6 losses, it is difficult to say that we experienced adversity. What we experienced was a low point or nadir in our journey. We had to solve some problems, get our heads on straight and begin playing up to our potential. As stated earlier, although the personnel didn't change, the team that won the national championship was not the same team including the coaches that started the season. Simply stated, the players experienced a coming of age.

There was nothing magic about this team. It all came down to work ethic, fundamentals, baseball intelligence, decision making and consistency. They were extremely well coached in fundamentals before they ever came to play with my team. They understood baseball better than most players at this level; more importantly though, they accepted ownership of their task. Simultaneously, they accepted the responsibility and held themselves accountable for their actions or inactions on the playing field. Nobody wanted to be the one who faltered and cost us a game.

They realized the importance of communication with each other on every play whether they were on offense or defense. They were able to stay focused, make good decisions and believed that they could handle any situation that might arise in a baseball game. To explain it, you need to understand that the real changes were not in the way our team made plays, it was in our mind set. All of the teams at this level of the tournaments could make the plays. What happened to our team was that, in the tight games, we were making better decisions than the teams we were playing against. We improved our decision making in pitching, on offense and on defense. The result was that we extended our innings on offense and cut their innings short. How does that look statistically?

Player	At bat	Runs	Hits	RBI	SB	Avg
Schell	77	18	33	12	17	.429
Andert	81	10	21	11	2	.259
Clarke	59	9	16	9	1	.271
Coker	60	20	20	13	11	.333
Vargyas	26	5	7	2	0	.269
Shepherd	72	10	20	17	3	.278
Heyde	57	7	13	8	4	.228
Yates	8	2	4	1	0	.500
Kowatch	59	13	15	4	5	.254
Romeo	39	8	9	7	2	.231
Szajko	35	13	15	4	5	.429
Madey	19	1	2	2	0	.105
Toles	8	0	1	2	0	.125
Hankins	9	1	0	1	0	.000
Janiszewski	5	0	1	2	0	.200
Rudasics	0	0	0	0	0	.000
Ross	0	0	0	0	0	.000
Team Totals	**614**	**117**	**177**	**95**	**50**	**.288**

These, however, are only half of the story. Our pitching staff put up even more staggering numbers in our eighteen game tournament winning streak.

Pitcher	Innings	Hits	ERs	Walks	K's	ERA	Wins
Rudasics	2-2/3	3	2	2	1	6.76	0
Yates	10-2/3	11	5	4	10	4.22	1
Jano	23	23	7	1	18	2.74	2
Hankins	59	35	7	14	53	1.07	7
Heyde	67-2/3	50	6	22	63	0.80	8

Needless to say our defense strongly supported our pitching by averaging only 1.2 errors/game, while making the right decisions, at the right time, on the big plays.

In many cultures there are rights of passage that males have to go through to be accepted as full fledged members of their tribes or communities. In Africa, it's the young warrior killing a lion. In American Indian lore, it is the young warrior killing a buffalo.

On this team it was each player coming of age in his own way. Some were very easy to discern, others were much more difficult to see. They all happened but they happened at different rates and in very different ways to each person. For them, being able to see their roles and accepting them was the biggest part of the transformation.

After the excitement of a season like the '77 season dies down and everything begins to sink in, the analyses begin to take place. Let's begin by saying that northern Indiana had a lot of strong players coming up at that time. Several would make it to the major leagues. Many had become legendary in the area and their names carried the rest of their teams with them into the baseball lore of the region. The initial comparisons were to other teams in the area that had very talented key players. Some of these teams had more than one player who went on to the majors or more players who went on to play at the Division 1 college level. Still others were teams that had more notoriety during the regular season. In other parts of the state people will compare their local teams with what they remember about our team. If they beat us during the year they're sure that we were lucky to get past them and not meet them again in the tournament.

The next step the aficionados take is to compare individual players. They'll look at our pitching staff and swear we didn't have one major league caliber pitcher much less a pitching staff talented enough to win. Yet our first and second pitchers (Greg Heyde and Dave Hankins) had identical records of 15 wins and 1 loss. That's a winning percentage of .938. Our team record was 41 and 6. That's a winning percentage of .872 for the season against the best possible talent in the country. However, as previously stated, in so many of the tournaments, they looked at our size and said what so many of our opposing teams said, that they were bigger than we were, hit harder than we did and had better arms than we did. That all may be true but as we progressed through the tournament it didn't seem to carry over into the games.

The most important truth, however, is that we are the team that went through the tournament and won the National Championship on the field. This isn't newspaper sports reporters' or active coaches' or judges voting. This is what happened on the playing field. College football is still looking for a playoff system. If there were teams that were better than we were that year, all they had to do was play us in the tournament and beat us on the field to prove it. One team's coach said that, although we beat them and every other team, they were still a better team than we were, and in fact we were probably no better than the third or fourth best team in that tournament.

Everyone is quick to make subjective comparisons with other teams from other years. All of the comparative teams had talent and coaching and in many cases players who later became major leaguers. The final differentiating factor was the outcome of their seasons versus ours. The truth of the matter here is that we are the only team from Indiana to have ever won the National Championship. Our overall record stands as stated; 41 wins and 6 losses and we went undefeated in 18 tournament games.

We couldn't have improved our tournament record if we did anything differently or even added any other players no matter how good they were. That being said then why did it happen to this team, at this time? Some will call it chemistry. Some will call it synergy. Some will even say that the stars in the sky all lined up for us and it was our year. Oddly enough nature did play a role. The rain delays we experienced were timely and beneficial in that they allowed me to use Greg Heyde and Dave Hankins more times than I would have.

One question that continually comes up is…"Didn't they get stressed out playing under all of that pressure." The answer is no, but this needs additional explanation. Pressure doesn't occur in nature. Pressure is self-created by the doubts we have about our own abilities to deal with a situation. A quote from basketball coach Bob Knight is germane to this explanation. "The will to win isn't nearly as important as the will to prepare to win." Knowing this, I can say without trepidation, our team was more prepared than those teams we played. I could see it in their expressions, their body language and most importantly in their performance.

My contribution to this team was that I didn't try to undo the coaching they had received before they got to me. I accepted what they brought with them. I was the first coach they played for that treated them as adults and as teammates, only with different responsibilities. I did teach them the importance of breaking a game down into its smallest controllable unit. I taught them to play one run baseball an inning at a time. They were also taught that as long as we had more innings left than we were runs behind our opponents, we had a more than even chance of winning the game. In addition I taught them what may be the most important lesson for life, how to lose with class and how to win with class.

During the season and especially during the tournament, we built the necessary relationships among the team members which included those on the field, those on the bench and with the coaches. Each coach and each player knew his role both on and off the field and trusted each teammate to know his. I believe we were able to do this because we were on the road, living together, those final three and a half weeks.

It's important to understand that managing and coaching this team isn't about me, it's about the players. I was the director and they the performers. I coached from the masters and patron point of view. I was the patron and they were the masters. Everyone remembers Michelangelo but nobody remembers Machiavelli. I provided the venue and the resources and they produced the work of art.

Years ago Tom Peters, made a presentation entitled, "In Search of Excellence." The definition of excellence is, something that gives special worth or value. It's almost like art, I can't define it but I know it when I see it. Just winning games isn't enough. It's how consistent you are when you play them and how you react to them after the fact. The Peters program made a mark on my professional life as well as my attitudes in coaching. Extending these expectations to this team was easy. I wanted and expected excellence both on and off the field from this team. This had to do with both playing the game and their deportment on the field and off. Teaching them how to lose with class and win with class were an integral part of it. Each man knew his role and my expectation of how he should achieve it. My Mission Statement with this team was the same that I held for my sales team; "To become so effective that we are a value to both internal and external customers."

As previously stated, it all begins with trust because trust changes people; they become what you tell them you expect. Fair and equal treatment builds trust. A coach should never put himself into a position where something he does might appear to be preferential treatment.

Every winning team has elite players and how you treat them creates the overall environment. A key point that a coach or a manager needs to bear in mind is that, when he has an elite performer he has to let him be that. He shouldn't give him added responsibilities; consistent performance demands all of his attention. Elite performers are natural leaders. Too many managers begin to formalize the roles of these players as team leaders. They want them to be "captains" or mentors. To begin with mentoring is a spontaneous connection between teammates. It has been my experience that this never works as an assigned function.

Elite performers have a greater impact when they are allowed to execute their skills on the field which usually creates a desire among their teammates to emulate them or at least to look to them, to ask them questions about how to improve their own games. What you don't need to create is an assistant manager or elevate a player above his teammates. This would create a negative environment not only for the team but for him as a player. When he makes an error, goes into a slump or simply has a bad game, his elevated level would continually be questioned.

No green lights should be given either at bat or on the base path. The key to success is that everyone needs to know what is going on all of the time. Green lights would negate that. Green lights with a few imply preferred status.

The impact this experience had on the coaches and players on this team can only be expressed by each of them individually. The memories of the experience and the reverence indicated by the descriptions each player makes about the season and his team- mates were surprising.

As Marc Toles so aptly described our change, "It was evidenced by a million different things; Bill Schell's unrelenting torment of opponents on offense and defense, Greg Heyde's complete imperviousness to pain, Jeff Coker's uncanny ability to read and remember pitchers that gave him an edge on every single pitch, and, of course, Dennis Janiszewski's unspoken attitude of win, smile and move on."

Others demonstrated their growth more overtly. Will Shepherd's hitting a home run in three consecutive games in the Indiana regional partly exemplified it. Inwardly, his real coming of age came when he took more of a leadership role after he replaced Gary Vargyas at second base at the state tournament.

Dave Hankins' giving up no runs in 20 innings on the mound in the Great Lakes Regional against two of the best teams in the nation, Morehead, Kentucky (9 innings) and Blissfield, Michigan (11 innings) was another example. It was here that he finally over- came his fear of making a mistake and realized how important he was to this team.

The change for Jeff Kowatch was even more dramatic. After routinely sitting during the regular season, he became a starter in the State Finals in Richmond, IN and more important than ever. He performed on both offense and defense as we advanced in the tournament. A squeeze bunt against Kentucky in Chicago gave us the only run of the game. His hit to right in the ninth inning against Illinois sent Heyde to the plate with the winning run. Two defensive gems in the National Finals were clear signs. "The Play" against California to get us out of the first inning holding them to only one run, and the throw to Schell who cut it and caught the runner at first who had rounded too far against Mississippi, decisively demonstrated his coming of age.

I am a charter member of the older I get, the better I was club but the one thing that each of these people can carry into his old age is an answer to the question, "How good a baseball player were you when you played?" The answer is unique in Indiana American Legion Baseball, "My team won the National Championship!"

BOTTOM OF THE 9TH

Our Post 50 team was special. Not so much individually, but collectively. We had some special players to be sure, some players who had special tournaments, but where we were the strongest is that we became a total team, in every facet of the game, on and off the field. It's the pack and the wolf thing; "The power of the wolf is the pack, but the power of the pack is the wolf".

It was our growth in becoming good friends, our maturation in becoming an unselfish unit, and our learning to assess very quickly what was needed at the most opportune times. Not because we were overly talented but because we were smart in terms of recognizing opportunities during our games. We seized moments and plays better than any baseball team I've ever been a part of.

Momentum is a funny thing. Fragile for some. Not for us. Once we had it and felt it, it was difficult for our opponents to overcome. We were never favored by the "experts". We had too many flaws according to the "book". There are no "experts" by the way; just so you know. And the "book" needs some revision. When you reach the point of total belief in yourself and your teammates, you are a dangerous team.

We've seen it before in baseball and other sports. Everyone wondering how this or that team winds up winning the championship against more formidable opponents. Stats, records, and number crunching are for people with too much time on their hands. Winning championships is for people and teams who aren't scared, and are tough enough to deal with whatever and whomever comes at them.

I must admit here that what we all felt and experienced together was uniquely ours. I don't know how many American Legion Baseball Teams have ever gone 18-0 or better in their state and national tournaments. I would guess very few, especially when you consider the modern era (post WW II). Say what you will, the bottom line is we never lost when it counted. Talented, lucky, opportunistic, it doesn't really matter in the end. They only put the ring on the winners' fingers.

It was very strange. We all could sense a feeling of loss when it was over. Yes, we were proud, exhausted, and in a groove of monumental proportion, but we also knew we would never play together again as a competitive force. There was a sadness to it that went unspoken. For those of us who continued to play in college, or on other amateur teams, we would have to try to create the magic with other teammates. For others who got a shot at professional baseball, I suppose baseball eventually became a business venture of sorts ultimately.

To be really good in baseball, to be the best, you have to have a host of skills. It's not easy. Some are gifted enough to make it look easy, but that's a ruse. They still have to make decisions in micro seconds and control their bodies enough to make plays. The physics of the game are truly amazing and make it very difficult to be a playmaker consistently.

You need to stand in the batter's box just once with a bat in your hands when a 90 + mph. rising or sinking fastball comes screaming at you in the blink of an eye to truly grasp the difficulty of the challenge. Or when someone hits the ball very hard at you with incredible topspin and it's on you in a blur and you have to make a decision on how to play it. The speed of the game is the craziest factor of all. Some say or believe baseball is slow. If that is slow, I don't want to experience fast. Courage…you better have a ton of it when you play the game at a high level.

When it all comes together for a team of young players like it did for us in 1977, the courage, the confidence, the momentum, the collective competitive spirit, it is something that you'd like to hand out to everyone like candy at Halloween. It's too good a feeling to keep only for yourself. But you can't give it to others. They must create it and earn it for themselves. Some will never possess the courage, for others their physical limitations will halt their climb to the top, still others don't want the work involved, and some just can't handle the pressure or the spotlight.

When I think back on what we accomplished as young baseball players, the physical things I will always take for granted. The hitting, throwing, catching, and running will always be the easy part. We were trained well, and we worked hard on those mechanical parts of our games. The real growth and what truly put us over the top though was the emotional and social maturation that took place that summer for each of us. We owe a big debt of gratitude to each other, our coaches, parents, opponents, and many others for the lessons learned that late summer and early fall. I just don't know if you can win like we did without the psychological stuff. There were obviously very talented teams throughout the tournament. Overcoming the talent of the opposition alone is too much for some. We craved it. We lived for it. You can't teach that to others.

Fast forward a couple of years to my sophomore year in college. I lose my championship ring on a golf course in of all places, Richmond, Indiana while golfing and partying, or I should say the other way around…partying and golfing with a friend from high school. I don't recall much championship level golf being played that day, at least not by us. I put my wallet, watch, and ring in my bag, like always. At the end of the round only my watch and wallet are to be found. Still have no clue. I took that bag apart, literally.

What shocked me was my ambivalence over the loss. I didn't get a replacement ring for close to 20 years. And it wasn't a money issue. I didn't need the ring, or all of the other nice gifts and memorabilia that we acquired to make me feel like a champion, or maybe more importantly to prove to others that I could play on a championship level against the best. Deep down, where nobody goes but me, I always knew that I could play like that, would play like that. Always. I just needed a place and time to show it. Mel, my talented teammates, and the summer of 1977 with Post 50 allowed me the opportunity to do that.

You can't buy that kind of self-esteem, you can't teach it to young people, and they can't have it handed to them by parents or coaches. They must earn it. It has to be acquired by them on their own, and preferably it shouldn't come too easily. There aren't too many naturals out there, in any endeavor. Most people will flinch at crunch time. We weren't naturals and we never flinched. We had most of the intangibles that are so elusive to teams and groups of people trying to achieve at a high level. Why us? We all had many outstanding people helping us along the way and we had all worked hard to hone our skills.

So when you reach the pinnacle of whatever you're chasing, you really appreciate your accomplishment and the people who helped you along the way. And there are usually lots of those folks that are never really thanked properly by the people who achieve goals. Once you achieve a major goal though, you always know that you have what it takes to do it again, even in another totally different environment. Confidence and poise are tough to master for some. For our team it seemed to never be an issue, especially after our mid-season nadir and refocusing. We never thought about it really. We just had "IT" from the beginning; even though we may have misplaced it for a little while. Our success only strengthened what we already knew about ourselves. That may sound trite or boastful to some. I don't mean it to. But through our home lives, athletic and school activities, our relationships, we had acquired a lot of "IT", whatever you want "IT" to be. I don't really know if one word can define it well enough, but athletes and coaches know what I'm talking about.

The great thing about the American Legion Baseball Tournament back in 1977 was the double elimination format. A great team could have one bad day per tournament and still advance to the next level. We didn't need the cushion. We didn't have any bad days. For five straight weeks we made good days every time we played, or at least good enough to win them all. Many of them were tight, highly contested, pressure-packed games, against outstanding competition. We took care of business each and every time we stepped onto the field. Our title was no fluke. We earned it. We also learned the value of capitalizing on momentum.

At the end of the day our story is simply this: We were an intelligent, extremely competitive group of youth baseball players who made the most of our opportunities. We learned to appreciate each other's skills and we evolved into a very effective TEAM. We all gave what we could on a consistent basis and blended our efforts together. It's called TEAMWORK. And along the way we had more fun than you could possibly imagine. That's the best part of all.

‟ ”

COKER #19

The 1977 Post 50 team was probably not the most talented team in the country, but we had something more valuable than talent. We had the exact ingredients for the chemistry and make-up of a baseball team that wins games. The manager of this team, Mel Machuca, was the catalyst in this mixture to produce the maximum results of winning from this team. Mel not only had the ability to choose the proper players for his team's mold, but also to place these players in the best position for the team's success. That includes both repositioning players in the field and lineup adjustments that I imagine took some players by surprise.

MADEY #12

The pitching staff was successful in my mind because each member stayed within himself. Each pitcher did what he could do and didn't try to do more. And when you have a solid defense behind you, that is really all that is required. No one was over confident and no one lacked confidence.

HEYDE #2

Maybe the key to our team was that we never panicked. The closer the game, the better we responded and the fewer errors we made. The coaching staff never gave us the idea that we were in a dilemma and Mel never let anything get out of hand.

HANKINS #14

There is a big difference between arrogance and confidence. Mel exudes the latter, which I think is the reason people trust him. People are also drawn to him because of his passion, which is reflected in his positive attitude and personality.

SCHELL #3

There isn't a lot I remember, but I will always remember the friends I made that summer, friends I will have for a lifetime. I thank God I had a chance to know such special people on and off the field.

TOLES #9

It wasn't perfection, but it was excellence. Excellence we achieved.
    Perfection is God's business.

EXTRA INNINGS

The Reunion Game

"If you can force your heart and nerve and sinew
to serve your turn long after they are gone
And so hold on when there is nothing in you
Except the will which says to them hold on."

R. Kipling

TOP OF THE 10ᵀᴴ

It's early June 1997 and again I'm going through near depression. I'm lamenting the fact that another summer has arrived and I have not taken the time to find a baseball team to coach. The last year that I coached baseball was in 1995 and that team was a group of fifteen-year-olds whose parents wanted their children to participate in a summer activity. They wanted a baby sitter. I really can't do that again. After all I've coached for twenty-three years in five different cities in four states and always at a higher level.

Just then the phone rings. It's Jeff Coker, the current baseball coach at Post 50. "Hey, Jeff, how are things going? It's been a long time since we talked. What's your team look like this year?"

"Great, I have a strong group of kids and I'm looking forward to the Tournament. How are you doing? Are you doing any coaching?" Jeff asks.

"No, not this year but I'll get back into it the first chance I get. So, what's up, Jeff?"

"Mel, it's been 20 years since we did it and I'm thinking, that we need a reunion." Jeff is, of course, referring to the year that we won the American Legion Baseball National Championship. In 1977 seventeen baseball players from Northern Indiana took me, Bill Barcome and Bob Kouts for a magnificent ride that started in South Bend in June and ended in Manchester, New Hampshire on Labor Day. We were the first team from Indiana to accomplish that and as it turns out the only one to do so to date.

"Jeff, I agree. It would be great to see everyone again." The oldest players on that team would now be thirty-eight years old and well into their careers and families. Thinking about that makes me realize how old I'm getting.

Jeff continues, "What I really want is to play a reunion game. All of us, the '77 Team, against this year's Post 50 team. Do you think we can pull it off?"

"I don't see why not. Have you contacted any one else?" I ask enthusiastically. He's grabbed my interest. I never really thought I'd have another chance to coach this particular group of players as a team again. I immediately start envisioning it in my mind. Jeff says that he's in the process of finding everyone. So far everyone he's contacted says he'll play.

As we continue I can sense that I'm speaking with a completely different Jeff Coker than the young sometimes arrogant 18 year old major league prospect. He's still completely confident in his approach to baseball, but has thoroughly changed in his interpersonal acumen. He's found an ability to empathize with other people's feelings. It is really demonstrated in one of his plans for the game.

"I want to do something else." He explains, "I want to dedicate an inning to Jano's memory. We'll announce him as 'Now pitching...' place his hat on the mound in the seventh inning, followed with two minutes of silence, and then announce 'That ends the inning because nobody could have hit Jano anyway!' then we'll go back to the dugout and continue the game."

Dennis Janiszewski died in 1996 in a tragic accident at a steel mill when a boiler exploded. I'm immediately moved by the mere thought of doing this.

Jeff goes on, "I'll supply the uniforms, hats, balls and bats. The only thing they have to bring is their spikes and gloves. We'll be playing at Coveleski Stadium, the new minor league ball park in South Bend. I can count you in then?"

"Absolutely! ", I answer.

"Great!" says Jeff. "I'll coach my team and play on your side a couple of innings during the game so I can hit."

So here we are a reunion game. I keep wondering what it would be like. I know my team has aged but I am equally sure that they are still in fairly good shape at least well enough to give me nine innings, or are they? I begin going through the list, Andert, Shepherd, Schell, Coker, Clarke, Kowatch, Szajko, Toles, Ross and Vargyas will be okay to cover the field, but how about catchers? I satisfied myself that Romeo and Madey could split the game, even if it has to be every other inning, so catchers are okay too. Now I have to think about the pitchers. Years have a way of wearing on arms and legs. We have Heyde, Hankins, Yates and Rudy. Jano is giving us one inning, even in his absence, so I have to get eight out of the other four. Heck, that's only two a piece. I reaffirm to myself that it won't be a problem.

I began searching my memory. Some things I didn't even have to look up. Forty –one wins and six losses, best year I ever had. The seventeen players on the team who evolved into the National Champions were difficult to separate into before and after person-alities. Remembering the individual turning points is harder but believe me, it did happen. Words like chemistry and synergy are often used to describe a great team. This team is no different but those words don't go far enough to describe or explain them or even what happened to them. When we were in the tournament at the highest levels, people kept saying "This is a once in a lifetime opportunity." That rolled off our ears because we were in the midst of playing. Besides that, I really didn't want to believe that.

I start looking forward to the Reunion Game. Coker tells me

not to worry about it. He'll set the lineup for me, all I have to do is coach third base and run the game on the field. I always thought that making out the lineup was one of my strengths, so that made me even more anxious. Positions in the batting order are keys.

My wife, Lynda, is chomping at the bit because she has lived with me through many baseball seasons including the big one and she's looking at this the way I am, as a chance to get back with this team just one more time. In the last two weeks of that memorable season, we spent more time with that team than any other team I had ever coached. Questions begin to arise, what if these guys have aged too much? What if they can't play anymore? Will they be embarrassed? Can we stop the game if it becomes too one-sided? Jeff assures me that he won't let that happen.

The ride to South Bend from Cleveland seems like it's taking all day. We finally arrive at the La Salle High School baseball field at about ten in the morning. Jeff Coker is there waiting for us, the rest of our team is trickling in one at a time, some with their wives some with their families hoping to catch a glimpse of the past aura that surrounded this team. Bill Barcome is there too, as he always is, ready to do anything I ask of him. We begin to prepare our game plan. This is the easy part. Our game plan never changes. One run per inning is all we need to put these young pups away no matter how good they are. Our key to winning is always defense anyway. We didn't make a lot of errors and this isn't even a worry in my mind. I remember that we work on defense almost all the time and in the close games I always think that if we can keep the ball in the park, it's going to be an out.

Jeff has hats for everyone with a much improved Marauder emblem; the ones we had made locally by a seamstress were cut and embroidered by hand. The new ones were embroidered by a computerized patch-making machine. It is the eye-patched, base-ball- faced pirate wearing a red bandana with a bat in his mouth on a navy blue hat with a red button and red accented ventilation holes. They are really first class!

The gray uniforms with navy and red trim, Jeff loans us to wear, are brand new and somehow magically fit the heavier out of shape bodies they surround. I wonder if these were specially ordered for this game. The only other equipment I need is a fungo bat. This was a standing area of contention between Jeff and me since he broke my fungo bat in 1977 against a light pole at the Babe Ruth Park in South Bend. Jeff hands me one.

I start hitting infield, as I always did and notice that even though they have lost a step, their hearts are still very much in it. Coker at third, Schell at shortstop, Shepherd at second and Jim Andert at first look pretty good. Both Madey and Romeo, our catchers, are standing at the plate feeding me baseballs as they had so often done years before. I forgot however that I am dealing with thirty-eight year old teenagers today. Their passion for the game has reverted to hitting. They have long forgotten the virtues of defense that they used so adroitly in the two eleven inning and three one-run games in Chicago and again in the games in New Hampshire at the American Legion World Series.

As each steps up to the plate, his swings emphasize the strength that each remembered having so many years before. I can't hear the creeks but I know they are there in some of them. Bat speed, the essence of hitting is somewhat blurred over the course of time. Szajko and Heyde are still playing and have maintained most of theirs. The others have lost much of theirs from shear inactivity and loss of muscle tone. Jeff Coker can still hit but he was so far above everyone else in bat speed that year that a loss of up to 25% would move him only slightly nearer to normal. A big question is still in our lead-off man's bat. Would Bill Schell be able to hit for average as he had done in those two years he played for us? I am sure the answer would be YES, not to worry.

In my own mind, I am wondering if I can still wield the fungo as I used to. Maybe not as far or as hard but I still have the direction. Looking from the inside out, I haven't changed even though everyone else appears to have. I quickly change my thoughts to the ones that carried me through that year. These are the National Champions. I'm not playing today, they are. My mind says call the plays, they'll execute as they always did, flawlessly, without question or hesitation. I have unending faith in them and absolutely nothing to worry about with these guys. I just need to forget that twenty years have passed since we last played together.

One inning at a time, one run at a time is definitely the way to go. Our mantra! I keep thinking about strategy but it hasn't changed. As long as I have more innings left than the other team is runs ahead of us, we can win. I must have said it to them a hundred times. One time Woody Miller even wrote about it in the paper.

My thoughts then go to defense. We have to shut them down defensively. That is really the difference between us and every one we played twenty years ago. In the state finals, in the Great Lakes Regional Tournament and in Manchester at the World Series, defense was our key to winning. Questions begin running through my mind. Is the agility still there? Not fully maybe, but it doesn't matter because I can see it in their eyes. They believe they can and will rise to the occasion as they did in all eighteen tournament games.

Woody Miller is here again to cover the reunion game. He is the local sports writer who traveled with us throughout the tournament in 1977. Woody was and is a realist. He doesn't have to say much, and today, I remember his every look and what they all meant. He says again, that we can do it one more time.

Bob Kouts our baseball chairman, now approaching 80 years of age, is still there and very much a part of the Post 50 program. He has another side of him that everybody knew because it earned him a nickname. They called him three-ball Bob. He had a rule that he would only use three balls in any game. It started years ago during one particularly rainy tournament in South Bend. He carried a towel around drying off the balls that had gotten wet on the field and would not throw a new one in. Tight, chintzy not really! It was and still is a matter of principle to Bob.

At the reunion game twenty years later Bob Kouts, appears to have been waiting for this day his whole life. He is totally accepting of the money it's costing to play this game at Coveleski Stadium, have a banquet and hold onto your seats, give a major league quality baseball hat to every player, parent, and family member or friend who attends the banquet, unbelievable.

The team is ready to play again and waits for my signal to take the field. They still believe in me and let me lead. I am still their coach as I was in '77. Yes we had the superstars and yes we had the supporting cast. The single most important paradigm that I was able to instill in everyone on that team was a very simple concept. There is a responsibility that is an integral part of being good and that is simply that you have to play well all of the time. I keep repeating it to them so they will remember and believe it, as they take the field. "Success is not an end point; success is a mode of travel." In today's game I am going to repeat it every inning, just as I did so many years ago.

I stare at this team of men and as if I were looking at a hologram moving from view to view, somehow I see them again as teenagers. At the same time I don't know what they see when they look at me. I can't help but wonder, "Which team is showing up today; the National Champions or an over thirty-five group who won't be up to the challenge?" I'm trying to take it all in as though I'm a wide angle camera lens.

Jeff proves to be a great host. He provides everything we need for the warm up. He provides us uniforms, balls and bats and a field to warm up on. He gives us a lot of encouragement and keeps it as light as he can, so in the event that the worst happens we won't be embarrassed. The most important thing he gives us in this game is another chance to relive the experience of playing together. Memories are running wild, but at some point we are going to have to take the field and play the game against "the kids".

Driving up to the stadium gives me goose bumps. I walk through the hallway inside and walk out to look at the field. It is as beautiful a venue as I could have hoped for. Parents, fans and in our case wives and families are already there The most profound thing however, is that the smells of baseball, leather, grass and pine tar permeate the air. The stage is set and we are as ready as we are ever going to be.

As the home team, we sit in the third base dugout and bat last. After our mandatory infield, we are introduced along with the 1997 Post 50 team to enthusiastic applause from our fans and polite, respectful applause from theirs. The National Anthem follows and we are set to go. After Heyde's warm up tosses we throw the ball around the infield just like we did twenty years before, sort of.

Right off the bat, both literally and figuratively, of their leadoff man comes a scorching ground ball to the right side of the infield toward our second baseman. An instant before Will Shepherd had squared his shoulders, bent his knees, slightly separated his hands and set his feet in anticipation of a hit ball coming his way. As the ball passes him he is seemingly frozen in time. He would have easily fielded that ball the last time we played together. This time the only thing that moved prior to the ball's going past him was his head as he watched it zip by. He recovers nicely and turns to receive the throw from our center fielder Dan Szajko. The hitter is held to a single. That hit sends our team a message that Post 50 "the Younger" is not going to let Post 50 "the Older" slide by today. The gauntlet has been thrown.

Thanks to Greg, who probably hasn't pitched since yesterday, we hold them the rest of the first inning and as the side is retired, magically the clock moves back twenty years and we are in a ball game. It was up and down. They would score a run and we would answer with a run. One of our runs even comes on a squeeze bunt from Shepherd that sends Szajko across the plate.

As we move through the middle of the game and haven't been overwhelmed yet I called out to the team to wait for me in the dugout. I look them straight in the eye and say to them very matter-of-factly, "We're going to win this thing!" After hearing that, it was as though they had just received a blast of oxygen because everyone got his second wind. It was a new game.

Schell and Szajko are playing like their old selves, both on offense and in the field. Everyone is clicking even Todd, number ½ our batboy who now at 6'6", is towering over everyone as he intermittently retrieves bats, even though he is completely enthralled in watching the game.

In the seventh inning with the score tied, Jano's hat is laid on the mound. An announcement follows that Dennis Janiszewski, our deceased pitcher and teammate is now pitching. After a couple of minutes of silence, Bob Nagel makes the following announcement "…no runs, no hits, no errors. " heck, no one would have hit Dennis anyway so the inning is over. It is a stirring tribute and brought tears to many eyes. His wife and family are all there to see it. Great job, Jeff!

The score is still tied and it isn't over yet. Post 50 "the Younger" again take's a one run lead in the top of the eighth and again we answer in the bottom of the inning scratching out the tying run. In the top of the ninth Heyde, who has pitched three times a week since he was nine years old, returns to the mound. As usual, he comes in throwing hard and holds them scoreless as he retires three in a row. That set the stage for us. With one on and one out in the bottom of the ninth Greg, deciding enough is enough, hits a clothes line shot that clears the left field fence giving us a 9-7 win and a huge sigh of relief.

Once again with this team, everyone plays and everyone contributes. Post 50 "the Younger," witnesses and is the victim of a renaissance, in a group of never-say-die ball players, who will be hard pressed to find enough words to explain what just happened. Coincidentally, this game extends our streak to 26 wins in a row.

It is now time to retire to the Post 50 Legion Hall, have a banquet and tell of the dragon we slew today and all those from past wars so many years before on our march to that once-in-a-lifetime achievement.

BOTTOM OF THE 10TH

Twenty years is a long time to be away from anything. Competitive baseball and all that it entails made it seem like one hundred years for some of us. This much was certain though. We were all excited for the opportunity to be together again and the reservations and anxiousness about trying to play competitive baseball against a bunch of in-shape, talented teenagers would just have to be dealt with. There was no escaping the myriad of feelings. This next challenge for us though would put a whole new perspective on various things such as diminished athletic skills, EMT service at the stadium, vanity, and exercise, just to name a few.

Jeff Coker, the current coach at Post 50 at that time, had come up with the idea of having a reunion game featuring the 1977 National Champions against his current Post 50 team at Coveleski Stadium. Almost our entire team would come back to play it again Sam, one more time. The news was out though…THE BOYS WERE BACK IN TOWN!

Hide the women and children, stock up on Ben Gay and various other medical supplies, dig in the basement, attic, or closet for the old glove and spikes, and get ourselves together gentlemen. It is difficult to describe the various levels of fear, embarrassment, humility, enthusiasm, and excitement that we all went through leading up to our big date with destiny.

Some guys were still playing competitive baseball, believe it or not, and at a very high level of competition and success too. Dan Szajko was playing on a nationally- ranked old guy team in Charlotte, North Carolina, where he then lived, with a bunch of ex-professional players. Greg Heyde had continued to pitch and play for a 30-and-over league in town for many years. He, up to this point in time, had always played competitive baseball in the summer time. Jeff Coker had played some and joined some teammates and friends of Greg's for the Old Guy World Series in Florida a few times also. As for the rest of us…

We met at LaSalle Field for some BP and fungo practice before the game. Our families and friends would meet up with us at the stadium for the game. The feelings we had were mixed. You could sense that the jacking around here was just some Freudian defense mechanisms kicking in. When everyone got their chance to hit and field though, it was Johnny Ballgame all over again. Even our coach, who was battling cancer at the time, had that old familiar look in his eyes. It was freeze frame – 1977. For all of us the intensity returned without much effort needed. No one wanted to embarrass themselves or their teammates. Most importantly, we wanted to win!

Remarkably, most of our team still had the brain synapses firing for the graceful game we all loved to play in our youth. It was the muscle memory where the problems became a little obvious. We knew what to do with our bodies, hands, and reflexes. The game doesn't change. What had changed for sure was the extra weight and slowed movements. It clearly caused some of us some frustration. This used to be so easy; no thought, no doubt, no fear. We all tried to make it look as good as we could but the rust was evident. For guys approaching 40 years old, I suppose we looked like we still had it, but the lack of quickness and speed in our movements was obvious, at least to us.

Upon walking into the stadium, the juices were definitely flowing though. The ambiance of baseball; the smells, the colors, and the sounds, were all so vaguely familiar to us. When we looked at each other in Post 50 uniforms again it was like an old movie where you've seen this all before. Could we actually pull this off? We all knew the real bottom line issue was winning, but safety, embarrassment, and our legacy were also in our minds as we warmed up. Don't think for a second that they weren't.

One of the most poignant tributes ever witnessed on a baseball field anywhere happened in this game. Jano had been tragically killed in an industrial accident at his steel mill the year before. We placed his hat on the pitchers mound for the 7th inning and went out to our positions on defense. Then we held a moment of silence after a worthy tribute to him as a friend and teammate was read by Bob Nagle, our public address announcer for this game. For the coaches and players on our team it hit us real hard. We were coming face-to-face with the realization that our teammate and schoolmate was no longer with us in an earthly sense. We all felt his presence there with us though. To say the least, it was difficult to get our emotions together again in front of a very public audience. We did not play a 7th inning. Jano was pitching that inning in our hearts and memories, and he retired the opposition in order, like usual, three up and three down. We knew the tribute was coming so we were somewhat prepared for it, but the reality of it, as we experienced it, proved to be very emotional. Through the entire game, but especially after the tribute, we all felt a sense that we should not and could not lose this game because of him. He was a part of our 25-game winning streak and championship, and we would just as soon like to keep him and us on a roll. So we only played eight innings of live baseball.

I'd like you all to think that my first inning "attempt" (a very loose description) at the very first batted ball of the game, hit by their very good leadoff hitter, was a ploy to give them a false sense of security. My backhanded wave at the ball that ended up in center field was NOT the start for myself or my team that I had been dreaming about for a month or so. I guess it was entertaining for some though, as my teammates have reminded me about it for the last 10 years quite often. Greg Heyde looked at me as if to say, "It's going to be a real long day if I can't let them hit the ball on the ground to that side of the infield".

My memories of that game are vivid for only a few plays though. I'd like to forget that first play for sure, but can't, and my teammates won't let me anyway, that much is for certain. The greatest memory though, maybe for all of us, is the home run hit by Greg Heyde real late in the game as we are making another one of our trademark comebacks. He smoked a pitch over the left field wall with me on deck. What great timing. Not only did Greg have the key hit for us but he pitched like he was 18 years old again when he was on the mound. He had great stuff, still. I felt the same bullet proof confidence, the same pride when he was standing on that mound with a baseball in his right hand. Dave Hankins gave us a great effort also, and did it while injured. He pulled a hamstring but gutted it out and did quite well considering. I believe Rudy also threw for us. At 38, for those guys to do what they did against a very good team of teenagers, it was extraordinary.

For the players who could still run pretty well and were in very good shape, I'd NOT like to thank you at this time. But I have to because you made a ton of plays for us to be able to continue our streak. We won with a great comeback effort 9-7, and many of us went to the Post after the game and reminisced well into the evening. I am thankful for that time together. A special thanks to Jeff Coker for making this happen.

Here's the really funny thing about the whole fungo bat affair on that 4th of July in 1977, I didn't find out the real reason Coker broke it until I asked him about it at our 30th reunion. It had absolutely nothing to do with anyone from Post 50. He told me he was so angry at the home plate umpire for calling a couple of strikes on pitches that were so clearly out of the strike zone that he was just steaming inside from that moment on until the moment he boiled over when Mel was giving us his talk. This guy was what I call a "hemisphere" umpire. If it was in the Western, he was going to call the pitch a strike.

It had nothing at all to do with his disrespecting Mel or what he was saying to all of us at the time. Jeff was a simmering volcano somewhere on Pluto. The rest of us were on Earth, in the dugout at Rockne Field, in South Bend, Indiana. It was tough for Jeff to concentrate on what Mel was saying from a million miles away.

Jeff Coker knew the strike zone as well as any teenaged player that I have ever seen, period. His ability to lay off pitches early in the at bat and get a hitters count was one of his best attributes. And then when pitchers were forced to bring the strikes it was just a treat to watch. He seemed to never get cheated on a swing, and I've never seen a player of that age hit the ball so consistently hard. Jeff was the original poster boy for being comfortable in the batters box and the biggest reason for that was his knowledge of the strike zone. Great hitters can control their aggression. Jeff did that extremely well. Thirty years later he still seems to have that going for him.

To be reconnected with these guys at Covaleski Stadium for

such a tremendous athletic accomplishment, and to be able to relive it a little bit that day was an incredible thrill. Not quite everyone could make it back to South Bend for the reunion game but we had a very good turnout and it was great just to be able to catch up with everyone after so much time had passed. As you can imagine, we had migrated to all parts of the state and country by 1997, and it took a lot of effort and planning to pull this thing off. One of the nicest gestures of the entire experience was when Mr. Kouts, our Post 50 Baseball Chairman, gave all of us the new and improved Machuca Marauder Post 50 Hat to wear for the game. Mine is still prominently displayed in my basement along with my other memorabilia from our Post 50 days.

The arms and the legs had certainly diminished for most of us in the 20 years since our championship, but our intensity for success, and the fun we have when we're around each other were ever present, as everyone who saw us that day could tell. It's difficult to define or describe to others. We always feel it and sense it. We were reminded that day that on baseball fields, we always know what to do and where to be at any given time. Real life is not so easy to direct.

We didn't want to leave the stadium that day to go back to reality. Our memories of Post 50 baseball are too rich, too pleasant. We had triumphed again and it brought back some tremendous feelings for all of us. Another moment in the sun, when you've resigned yourself to the fact that it was over for you a long time ago, was a much welcomed rejuvenation for many of us. Just to connect with playing baseball again in a competitive environment was so moving. The receding hair lines, the bellies that were over the belts a little too far, and the creeks in the joints of our bodies, were just part of the living that we had done in the 20 years since our special summer baseball season. We got to see everyone's children, their brothers, sisters, and parents again, and it was like old home week, and we all enjoyed that tremendously.

BELLVILLE ATHLETIC COMPLEX – South side of town (My side by the way).

I was in the stands at a Post 50 game after our reunion with a couple of my teammates and the lady behind us is a mom of one of the current players, and she asked us if we were some of the guys that played in the reunion game and we said yes. She said to us that she couldn't believe that we could actually still play and beat a bunch of 18 year olds, a bunch of good 18 year olds. (This 1997 Post 50 team would play in the Indiana State Finals later on that summer). I remember trying to be polite and saying that it was a little unfair because we didn't have to see Jeff's top pitchers to which she replied, "Honey, I don't care who we had pitching. It's just not right for you guys to be able to do what you did. I would like to have seen you guys play when you were young." We said thanks and I remember feeling old for really the very first time around a ball field. Middle age is not old on the total scale of age but watching young men in the prime of their youth play baseball will age you quickly. It's the speed and the stamina.

Because of coaching the game, I can trick myself into thinking that I never really get old if I stay close to the game. But I am and our team is too. 1977 was a long time ago in most respects. In my mind's eye though, it seems just a little over about eight life times ago. And then it doesn't sometimes seem so long ago. I'll see one of my players, or a game on TV, and it will remind me of someone on our team, or a play someone once made in Chicago or somewhere else on the road. We used to be 18 you know; just the other day, and could run like that…and throw like that…and hit like that…

The competitive nature of the players on our team is what I'll always take away from that day in the end. Old, slow, and hurting; but we still had some left in the tank. We still could swing the bat enough, run enough, and throw well enough. It's what we were all praying and hoping for as that anticipated weekend arrived. There is always a lot to be said for some things staying the same.

“ ”

MADEY #12

My main concern was the hammies and groin. Throwing and catching didn't seem to be a problem, although several were complaining that the rust on the arm was so thick that a gallon of WD - 40 wouldn't help.

HEYDE #2

Things I remember about the Reunion Game;
- How happy I was to play with you guys and healthy enough to participate
- How loud the ball sounded hitting the catcher's mitt in that almost empty stadium
- Hitting a home run that finally didn't get overshadowed by one of Coker's bombs
- Our faces when we won again.
- Feeling 18 all over again
- Seeing the look on those kid's faces after getting beat by us and knowing they deserved it.
- My kids telling me that was the coolest thing they ever saw, and feeling proud again.

The biggest thing about that day was remembering Jano. I believe everyone wanted to win that game for him. I only played with him one summer, but I have a lifetime of memories he left with me. In the movie <u>the Last Samurai</u>, the Emperor of Japan asks, "Can you tell me how he died?" Tom Cruise answered, " No, but I can tell you how he lived."

SCHELL #3

My last thought that really sticks out, is the reunion game, we went into the game just to have fun, but after a couple of innings when we were still competitive, I saw that old fire. We were going to win that game. I saw that look in Heyde's eyes and everything was going to be OK.

Epilogue

"A last look"

TOP OF THE INNING

What propels ordinary people to do extraordinary things is a question for the ages. I know I can't answer that, so I won't try. I will, however, offer a possible broadly stated explanation of the metamorphosis that took place with our team. Not only did their play and focus improve but more importantly their decision making improved.

I manage my baseball teams and sales teams in the same way. I have four axioms:

1. "Don't let the things you can't do get in the way of the things you can do."[J. Wooden]
2. "The will to win isn't nearly as important as the will to prepare to win." [Bob Knight]
3. "The power of the wolf is the pack, but the power of the pack is the wolf." [R.Kipling]
4. Do it now. [Mel Machuca]

What seemed at the time to be a natural extension of a very good baseball season had suddenly become through our accomplishment, a story worth telling. Most of this team started out at tryouts not knowing where they would fit into the group. Our returning players were more confident; they at least thought they knew where they were going to play. It was the new players that experienced the anxiety that comes with new beginnings. They weren't sure if they were even going to make this team much less break into the starting lineup. It was the coming of age of this group of exceptional young men who had started the year out as teenagers and through an individual maturation process capitalized on a window of opportunity and became a championship unit.

What happened to the players on this team during this transition psychologically, I leave to others to determine. I was only able to measure the changes through their behaviors on the field or in the dugout that I could see. They appeared to be more confident and more able to control the way they played and the way they addressed the situations that confronted them as individuals and as a team.

The motivation for playing on our team was varied. Some were looking for a chance to earn a scholarship, others already had one and were looking for a competitive place to play to improve their skills. Others were hoping to get a chance to become professional baseball players. All of them wanted to play their best level of baseball and possibly win a championship on the way. Many had something to prove to themselves; that they could play well enough to keep up with the elite players in the area and throughout the state.

The players we had in that era were dedicated to the game. In their high school programs they were participating in an extracurricular activity. In American Legion Baseball they had to make a serious commitment in time and effort to play in a primary activity. They also had a financial commitment because of time away from a summer job. Our team in 1977 traded the entire summer because we played from Memorial Day to Labor Day.

At the twenty-year mark, we played a reunion game and realized that we were still enmeshed in the passion for the game. In 1977, most of the players experienced an immediate impact in the form of self esteem and personal confidence. Some were able to renew that feeling in the reunion game. Winning that game only put that game categorically in among the other tournament games we played throughout that 1977 season. There we were too small, too slow etc… only this time we were too old to play against our opponent. We were too unpracticed, too out of shape, and too many pounds overweight. Our arms were weaker, our legs were weaker and it had simply been too long since most of us had played or even touched a bat or a ball. Somehow we extended our winning streak to 26 and again it was in the last inning. How do we explain the outcome?

Thirty years later it is difficult to find the same level of commitment. Travel teams are actively recruiting the more talented players. Many of them have substantial sign up fees and promise limited or no practices and a guaranteed number of tournament games. It seems that nobody wants to work for the prize anymore. Of the many things I've noticed over the years in sports is that people don't want to earn something on an even playing field, they want an advantage or a guarantee out front. They don't want to accept the responsibility for the outcome.

In 1977 everyone grew as the tournament progressed. Our play improved, and our decision making improved and it was this that separates very good teams from great teams. Players realizing and accepting their roles is an aspect of this game that cannot be overestimated. It is also something that you can only recognize after the fact if you are not the one doing it. The most effective way for this to be determined is by the individual player himself recognizing the role and going through the four A's: acknowledge, assess, adapt and adopt it so that he can turn it into an added value for the team. The players on this team did that.

The changes the players on this team experienced as a result of playing for and winning the National Championship was a visible expansion of them as individuals. I witnessed it in their growth on the field in the Tournament, again right after the Championship game and partially in New York City where we attended the MLB World Series. It wasn't in inflated ego or conceit, it was in their self-confidence. Although many of the players left for school immediately following the tournament, I could see it on their return to the banquet in December.

Needless to say the returning players will take this growth with them to their next year. Marc Toles, Dave Yates, John Ross, Dan Szajko, Dom Romeo and Scott Madey were definitively more mature than they were at the start of this year. It's on the field where this change will be most discernable to others, but more importantly it will show up in other aspects of their lives when they need it.

As I said earlier, after we won the championship I began thinking about more involvement in the state's baseball program and it took several years but in 1980 we finally got our chance. It was at the Indiana state American Legion mid-winter conference in Indianapolis. The incumbent 3rd District baseball chairman wanted out. Our Baseball Chairman, Bob Kouts, and I went hospitality room to hospitality room throughout the hotel courting votes. This was an intoxicating feat because we had to have a drink in every suite we entered.

It was getting late and the only thing that could possibly compete with the politics of American Legion Baseball was food, so we went to the famous St. Elmo's Steak House to eat. We ordered and were served and I wanted to talk with Bob about the election the next morning but he was, I'm sorry to say, slightly under the weather. He, of course, denied it because he knew he could hold his beer. I asked him at that point, "Then why are you trying to cut your steak with the ear piece of your eyeglasses?" He harrumphed, put on his glasses, picked up his knife and finished his steak. We finished eating and went back to the hotel to get some badly needed sleep.

At the baseball meeting the next morning, Taxi Ayres, the State Baseball Chairman, announced that the new 3rd District Baseball Chairman was Bob Kouts, I leaned over and poked Bob in the ribs to wake him up as he had fallen asleep in his chair and missed the announcement. That's why I loved this man; having a team participate in the program was more important than any personal recognition or position he might gain.

BOTTOM OF THE INNING

Many other teams have won American Legion Baseball National Championships. The National Tournament has been around a long

time, beginning in 1926. Where we rank on that list of championship teams we do not know. Nor are we looking for any analysis or
comparisons with them, or any other teenage championship teams
for that matter. In the telling of our story, one of our main goals
was to allow readers to wrap themselves around this one unmistakable fact - extraordinary success can happen to ordinary people
and teams. They just have to make the most of their talent and
opportunities. Our baseball team was ordinary in many ways;
extraordinary in a few that really mattered.

We didn't invent competitiveness, mental and physical toughness, teamwork, or delivering at crunch time. Though we were
keenly aware of what we needed to do and how we needed to play
to keep advancing in the tournaments. And that's from an individual, as well as a team perspective. Having the ability to do it is
only a small part of it. We played against many teams and players
who had more than enough ability.

The point here is we were an "Every Man" kind of youth baseball team. Yes we had some talent, but it was relative compared to
some of our opponents in the American Legion State and National
Tournaments. We were like so many other teams from across America,
the kind you might see anywhere; very good and getting better with
every opportunity. Believe me, there were teams that were eliminated
in their State and National Regional Tournaments that had enough
talent to win the National Championship. They just didn't. We did.
That simple. No secret potions, no magic formulas.

What may be THE key component to our entire success story
and experience is sagacity. By definition sagacity is the intelligent
application of knowledge. Our Post 50 team had it and demonstrated it throughout the tournament. We used the two tools that
everyone has, our brains and our past experiences, to help us in
our quest. We absorbed effectively what our previous and current
coaches, teammates, and opponents had taught us about the game.
We then used that knowledge to meet and defeat our challenges.

No one on our team ever played a single inning in the Major
Leagues. Actually, only two teammates of ours signed professional

baseball contracts; Jeff Coker, our power hitting third baseman signed a free agent contract with the Phillies just a few days after we returned home from New Hampshire, and his high school team-mate, Dan Szajko, after being drafted five years later signed with the Expos following his senior year at the University of Notre Dame.

One could argue that our team and individual deficiencies were somewhat of a burden to us, holding us back from changing the perceptions that seemed to follow us around to all of the tournaments. Gaining respect and changing the perceptions of others are over-rated sometimes. Even winning championships doesn't guarantee it. Of the many life lessons that Mel taught us that summer, not dwelling on our limitations was a big one. Do what you do well and do it better than others. He also taught us to break up the big goal into attainable smaller ones. We did exactly that, 18 times in a row.

An inning at a time!

｢｢ 〞〞

ANDERT #7
We always thought about getting better the next game ...the next inning...the next out. The winning and losing "really" isn't as important as the effort, the preparation and the dedication put into the game. This was tough to acknowledge but became easier with age and my having to admit to my diminishing skills in athletic endeavors. However, those same traits applied to everyday life, effort, preparation, and dedication will serve one well in the game of life.

COKER #19
One of the ingredients that is needed to make a championship team is quite often unnoticeable to fans and opposing teams. Only

our players knew the invaluable asset of every player on this team. With only nine available spots open, it meant someone who had the ability to contribute to winning wasn't going to get much of a chance during tournament play. We had totally capable players who accepted that role without complaining, bickering, or hoping somebody didn't perform well so they would get an opportunity. Even though all our teammates wanted that chance to contribute, never once did I sense anything but guys sacrificing for the good of the team. I have been on other teams that did not have that same team unity. Those teams seem to have more selfishness and that eventually led to the demise of that team reaching their potential. My hat is off to these players who I consider the consummate teammates.

TOLES #9
That summer was one of the greatest experiences I have ever had. It has added to my life immensely, in ways that have less to do with baseball and much more to do with life itself. It gave me a frame of reference for so many things, good and bad, that I have been faced with since.

It is also one of the most difficult things I have been through. I loved and respected every man on that team, and, especially, the man who led us. I wanted desperately to be on the field with them contributing something more than a nice clean scorebook. But I knew that everyone was doing exactly what he was supposed to be doing, and that I could either play my role as well as my teammates and my coaches were playing theirs, or I could regret it the rest of my life.

A tough pill to swallow at 17, but I was surrounded by some really tough guys who taught me well. I wouldn't have traded that summer for more playing time anywhere.

VARGYAS #15
After the Regional in South Bend I took off for Purdue, football was starting and I hated to go. To this day I feel a little bit removed

from your accomplishments because I wasn't there to participate with you during the great run. I called home every day after doubles to see how you had done. It all worked out and when we had the banquet you made me feel part of the whole experience, I thank you all for that.

KOWATCH #1
We were a team that made plays at the right times under the greatest of pressures. At times it seemed miraculous. Victory and success, to me, are always so humbling. They are never guaranteed and are never deserved. There are so many things in a game or in life that we cannot control, but we did take care of the things we could control. We showed up, were ready to play when it counted, made the great efforts and trusted each other.

HANKINS #14
We didn't reinvent the game. Our strategy was brilliant in its simplicity. It involved applying our knowledge of the practical principles in conjunction with basic fundamentals—theoretically, playing the game the way it is supposed to be played.

SCHELL #3
Lastly, as I look back now, the greatest thing I got out of the whole experience is the credibility it gave me with my son. There is no greater thrill than seeing a son grow in the game you love!

ROMEO #13
I took my daughters to Cooperstown a few years back and found the Legion area and it just says South Bend Post 50 - 1977 - IF THEY ONLY KNEW!

I cried when I saw it - then I laughed - then walked down the hall and saw Ruth - Aaron- etc, etc - and thought, bet they never won 25 games in a row when they were 17!

Appendix 1

PLAYERS

1 Jeff Kowatch – Pitcher/ Right Field 5'8 ½ " 150 lbs. Bats Right/Throws Right

Originally a second baseman or shortstop, Jeff played an intelligent game and completed our outfield as soon as I moved him out there. He never seemed or played as though he were out of position because he had good instincts and good arm strength. Jeff had a great eye at bat, never missed a sign and came into his own in the Great Lakes Regional against Morehead, KY when he stretched as far as he could to reach an outside pitch and laid down a perfectly executed squeeze bunt. We won 1-0. "The Play" happened against Santa Monica in the World Series when he used his leg to push off of the right field fence after a catch and whirl around to double the runner at first holding them to a single run in the 1st inning. We won 7-1.

Played baseball and basketball at Grace College.

(Quote) … "I remember after the weekend in Indianapolis (Beach Grove) that I thought this team was going nowhere. The thing I learned from that point on was the importance of commitment, perseverance, and faithfulness."

2 Greg Heyde – Pitcher/Left Field 5'8", 160 lbs. 15 wins -1 loss Workhorse

Second in HRs with 6. An iron man with a rubber arm. He was a wrestler in high school and college and was the strongest small man I had ever seen. Paul Eitler, coach at Post 357 released him in an unselfish move to allow him to play for us. His pitching stamina was unparalleled. I didn't like his swing because it seemed as though he was always trying to lift the ball but it worked for him so I learned how to live with it. Greg was number one in the rotation but I used him as a stopper several times. His real strength was his confidence. Greg was the original "Put me in coach, I can do it!", and I believed him. He played left field when he wasn't pitching. He shared it with Yates and Shepherd. I saw him as one of our tough guys but he became a stabilizing influence both on and off the field.

Greg attended St Joseph College in Rensselaer, IN

(Quote) …"I've been graced in life by this game of baseball .I've played with exceptional athletes and have been mentored by some of the finest coaches .I've made friends and have memories that will last a lifetime. I've been lucky enough to be affiliated with one of the best American Legion teams in the country for 30 years. Thank you guys!"

3 Bill Schell – Shortstop – 5' 9" 145 lbs.

All State HS, All American –2nd Base Texas Wesleyan University

Hillerich & Bradsby Hitting Award .441 National Tournament -American Legion Player of the Year 1977

His fundamentals were impeccable, his baseball appetite voracious but the irony was that he was as patient with those around him as anyone I've ever coached. He defined his role on the field and his role with me. He also defined my role with him. I led him because he let me lead. He knew that this game needs total communication. He was the foundation of our team and our drawing card.

On defense; positioning, relays, cutoffs and double plays were his to control and as the team leader, he did. He was always on base and wreaked havoc on opposing pitchers and fielders.

Eight for nine in the first two games of the World Series.

(Quote) ... "The National Regional was the most intense round of baseball I have ever experienced. I think that is where we became 'The Team'. It was a total team effort."

4 Dan Szajko – Center Field 5'8" 150 lbs.

The "player to be named later" that came with Romeo from Lenny Buczkowski, the Adams High School baseball coach, that turned into a bonus. Dan Szajko, the only sixteen year old on the team. Strong arm, great baseball sense and immediately was an asset; the second fastest on the team next to Schell. Dan never seemed to feel pressure and at sixteen that is really saying something. At bat he had a great eye. From the time he joined us I felt that he belonged with this group. He arguably was one of the most intelligent on the team. His speed made him an instant threat on the base path.

5 for 5 in first two games of state finals.

Became a 3-year man with Post 50; also played for University of Notre Dame and professionally in the Montreal Expos Organization.

(Quote) ..."Overlooked, underestimated, underdogs, or over- achievers; label us any way you like. We played and won as a team on the field against all of our opponents. The one thing that you should call us is winners."

5 Mike Clarke – Pitcher / Center field – 6' 175 lbs

Good speed. Strong arm with great instincts both offensively and defensively. His head was always in the game and he was a fundamentally sound player. Initially thought he was going to be a standout pitcher and the anchor of our pitching staff, but an injury to his shoulder kept that from happening. I liked his form as soon as I saw him, He had a fastball an overhand curve and a changeup that made him hard to hit. Offensively, he was a solid contact hitter; he made things happen when he was at the plate with men on base. He was deceptively fast on base and in the outfield, maybe because he always got a great jump on the ball. He brought leadership and maturity. In a very unselfish move, at the National Finals he came to me before a game and said he was not one hundred per cent and thought that I should start Szajko in his place. He came back the next game at 100%.

(Quote)… "No play changed all of our lives more than the last pitch and the last catch in the last game."

6 John Ross – catcher 5'8" 155 lbs.

Didn't play as a senior at Clay High School which placed him at a disadvantage because he was starting three months and thirty games behind those who played high school ball in 1977. Was always willing to work hard and would play any-where I needed him. Just being on this team with this group of players forced him to play at a higher level. John would give you one hundred per cent effort every day. He seemed to understand our opportunity from the beginning and wanted to be a part of it. He was a team player with controlled enthusiasm. He looked to the leaders and became a solid team player.

(Quote)… "Hey, I don't care what you put in the book, as long as you tell people I hit a home run in Warsaw."

7 Jim Andert – First Base 6'3" 170 lbs.

One of the first people whose position I changed permanently but as a convert from 2nd base to 1st base his learning curve was almost immediate. He was a big target had great fielding skills and became a stabilizing influence. He had great mental acuity which made him a great number 2 hitter. Patient beyond his years and thoroughly understood that he had to give our leadoff man, Bill Schell, time to work his magic on the bases. He had a great sense of humor with strong interpersonal skills and he helped to keep everything light in the dugout. Nothing got through him, not throws, not grounders or line drives and his head first dives on the bases brought ratings of 9.9 even from the Russian judge. Played at Ball State University.

(Quote)… "'It looks like a line drive in the scorebook.' As a team I think we also adhered to that motto. Just doing whatever it took to make the play, move the runner along or take an extra base."

Jeff Rudasics – Pitcher 5' 11" 170 lbs.

Part of the pitching trio from Clay High School with Hankins and Janiszewski. Well coached and fundamentally sound, he was number five in our eight man pitching staff He was a fine location pitcher and understood how moving the ball kept the hitters off balance. He came in relief against Elkhart the second time we played them. They opened the game by scoring 4 runs in the first inning and led 5-1. Rudy, in relief, strikes out two to end the inning and leaving Elkhart with the basis loaded. We won 6-5. He followed with a 6-0 win at Whiting in our last regular season game. He was important to the team not only on the field but also to our team culture and cohesiveness. He had strong relationships with the entire team and his sense of humor helped everyone to relax and maintain a positive attitude. Pitched at Huntington College.

(Quote)... "While the day started out with our being backed to the wall, it may have been the greatest moment in sports history when we came back and beat Arlington Heights."

9 Mark Toles – First Base 6′2″ 170 lbs.

Originally a shortstop, he would fit in wherever I needed him without hesitation or question. This was Marc's second year and he knew my coaching style and what I expected from him. His move to first came as a result of the number of middle infielders we had. He was tall and slim and made and accepted the position change to first base with enthusiasm. This was a key switch because he wasn't used to playing the game from that side of the field.

His knowledge of baseball made him an asset to the team.

(Quote)... "It wasn't perfection, but it was excellence. Excellence we achieved.

Perfection is God's business."

10 Dave Yates – Pitcher / Left Field 6′ 5″ 190 lbs.

Yates was and looked really big out there. He had a big windup and a straight over the top delivery that was intimidating to hitters. His fast ball jumped left and right as it came in. He also had a good hard breaker to offset the fastball and like the rest of the staff, he had good control. He had our third best record and was the only seventeen-year- old on our pitching staff. I had to lean on him when Janisewski broke his finger and he rose to the occasion. He didn't throw aspirin tablets, he threw disintegrating peas. On defense he also played left field which gave me a great feeling of comfort when considering the strength of the arms in our outfield. Pitched at Bethel College.

(Quote)... "The whole tournament experience is one that will never be forgotten. It marked so many firsts in my baseball endeavors such as flying on a plane for the first time, being away from home for an extended period of time, being asked for an autograph, standing at home plate in Yankee Stadium."

11 Will Shepherd – Pitcher / Second Base 5'7" 160 lbs. Third in home runs with 5.

Our only three year player. He analyzed the game both offensively and defensively. I batted him at cleanup, fifth or sixth. He was keenly aware of the benefit of facing pitchers who always seemed to be pitching to him from the stretch. Pitched and played the outfield and found a home at 2nd base at the state finals playing there through the rest of the Tournament. An extremely difficult switch since he was moving to the opposite side of the playing field. He was cognizant that he was playing next to Bill Schell and with him improved our double play combination. He came into his own at the state regional where he hit three home runs in three games. Definitely a team leader. Went on to Play at Butler University and coach the Varsity Baseball Team at Warsaw High School.

(Quote) ..."The most impressive gift we all gave to each other those five weeks was passion; for the game, and for each other"

Scott Madey – Catcher 6′ 1″ 170 lbs.

With Scott, we had a catcher. He was a strong receiver. I knew he had bad knees but after the season started they never seemed to bother him, if they did he kept it to himself. I often wondered what was going through his mind as we looked for a second receiver. He missed his junior year of high school ball due to surgery but was fundamentally sound. In addition to calling an intelligent game he was alert to everything that was happening on the field. He had a decent arm and was a good contact hitter and let me know what was happening whether he was playing or on the bench. He read opposing pitchers as well as he read our own.

(Quote)… "Our pitching staff? They were good! They weren't looking to strike everyone out. Knowing they had an excellent defense behind them, they were content with staying within their game, making their pitches and being very effective."

Dom Romeo – Catcher 5′ 9″ 150 lbs.

Dominic was seventeen and one of the seniors on his high school's summer team. The fact is that we needed a second catcher. He came to us with "a player to be named later." Our schedule demanded two catchers because of double headers and because of the level of our competition. I was willing to have a number one and a two but as it worked out we ended up with two number one's.

He was agile and an excellent receiver and had a more than adequate arm. Dominic was fundamentally strong and called an intelligent game. Against John Newman of Terre Haute(14 strikeouts) in the State Finals he stroked a home run that surprised everyone and opened the game up for us. Played at Manchester College.

(Quote)..." My biggest memory was seeing every pitch from the vantage point I had watching you all win."

Dave Hankins –Pitcher - 6' 1" 170 lbs

North-South All Star Game- Legion 15 wins-1 loss

One of our two workhorses; he registered 20 shutout innings in the Great Lakes Regional in 9 and 11 inning complete games. Then followed it with a one run complete game in the National Finals against the defending National Champion. His best pitch was a slider and given the fact that he could throw it where the catcher asked for it Madey and Romeo called it often. His slider would come inside and bend to hit the inside corner. When thrown on the outside corner it would bend moving slightly out of reach of the hitter. This allowed him to throw his fastball which the hitter would take because he didn't want to look foolish swinging at a pitch fading out of his reach. Pitched at Westminster College in Missouri.

(Quote)... "Winning the Championship was incredible, but the fact that we held up under the pressure was even more amazing, and like everything else, we did it collectively."

15 Gary Vargyas – Second Base 5' 10" 195 lbs.

A second-year player who played the game with a great deal of passion. Defensively he had limited range but his enthusiasm made up for it. He concentrated on hitting and was a good contact hitter and hustled all of the time. He was also a spark plug and had the ability to fire things up when they started to get too quiet. A head-on collision with the catcher in our first sectional game against Elkhart knocked the

185

ball loose and he scored but it set off a tirade from the Elkhart coaches and fans that led to their leaving the field in protest. We were winning 6-4 at that moment in the game and the protest was not upheld. Gary who had done a good job for us all year left us to play football for Purdue University just prior to the state finals.

(Quote)..."*I took off for Purdue, football was starting, but when we had the banquet you made me feel part of the whole experience, I thank you all for that.*

17 Dennis Janiszewski – Pitcher 5' 9" 180 lbs.

He really wanted to be part of this team and he wasn't going to let a broken bone steal the opportunity. He could feel the talent this team had and he knew he had to be part of whatever happened. He broke a finger on his throwing hand in the third game of the season sliding back into first. His curve ball could move three feet left to right with a drop in altitude of 6-18 inches. It was a killer and would drive hitters crazy. His 9- inning complete game against Hattiesburg in Manchester was a masterpiece. Pitched for Huntington College.

An industrial accident took his life in 1996.

(Quote)... "Jano's unspoken attitude of win, smile and move on."
-- Mark Toles.

19 Jeff Coker – Third Base 6' 180 lbs. All State Signed -Philadelphia Phillies

Led team with 13 Home Runs.
Arguably the premier hitter in all of Indiana that high school season. A one-swing game breaker. He didn't hit the long ball. The ball literally exploded off of his bat. The three furthest home

runs I have ever seen hit by an amateur or a professional were hit by Jeff Coker. In an Adams High School Baseball game when he hit a ball over the left field fence over two tennis courts onto the roof of the school, in Richmond, Indiana at the State Finals when he hit a light standard nearly ninety feet high sitting in front of the 497 foot mark and in Chicago at the Great Lakes Regional, he tried to hit it into the pool beyond a lawn well over the center field fence. He was 7 for 9 in state finals.

(Quote)... "One of the ingredients that is needed to make a championship team is quite often unnoticeable to fans and opposing teams. Only our players knew the invaluable asset of every player on this team. My hat is off to these players who I consider the consummate teammates.

½ Todd Machuca – Batboy 4′ 5″ 60 lbs. 7 years old

My original reason for coaching baseball was to get Todd, my son, interested in playing. It didn't work, he grew to 6'6" and ended up playing hockey, basketball and soccer and later volleyball.

During the Great Lakes Regional game against Arlington Heights he approached the plate to retrieve a bat but he had a snow cone in one hand and popcorn in the other. He knew he couldn't pick it up so he kicked it and returned to the dugout. Moments later it was announced on the PA system that he set an individual record for most trips to the concession stand.

Just his presence did a lot to soften the intensity of the games.

(Quote) ... "I need some money to go to the concession stand."

THE COACHES

25 Bill Barcome American Legion Baseball – 1977 Coach of the Year

First base coach. Called and won three of four coin flips in the National Finals. Easy to work with bought into all of my strategies and tactics. Willing to do anything at a moments notice. Additionally, he was comic relief personified. As the first base coach he had to read all of my signs from across the field and if a man were thrown out at second, missed a sign or even worse got picked off first base, he instinctively knew that he was going to catch heat from everyone on the team. Those are the times when he wished he had an asbestos uniform. He really helped to soften the intensity of the game.

(Quote)... "It wasn't my fault!"

Dan Toles Bench Coach throughout the national tournament.

Joined us at my request on very short notice at years end. Backed everything we did and had an upbeat attitude. Had previously coached at the younger levels and served as President of the Babe Ruth League (13-15 yr olds) in South Bend. Brought a sense of calmness with confidence to our dugout and made it seem as though he had been with us throughout the season.

(Quote) ... "Knowledge is something we learn, wisdom is what we do with our knowledge. This team's wisdom came from their talent and knowledge, and they demonstrated it by winning at all levels"

Mel Machuca American Legion Baseball- 1977 Manager of the Year

Served as fund raiser, scheduler, and recruiter. Also served as leader, motivator, mentor and coach. Taught the team to break the game down into the smallest component part; to play one-run baseball an inning at a time. Taught them how to lose with class and win with class. Moved people to understand that they were responsible and accountable for what they did on the field. Built a winning culture into the program. Also taught them that success is not an end point but a mode of travel. Trusted the team and got the team to trust him. Coaching is all about relationships. Playing is all about fundamentals and decision making.

(Quote) … "Trust changes people; they become what you tell them you expect."

VIPs

Bob Kouts Two fisted, beer drinking, cigar smoking, right hander Dugout Coach -Baseball chairman, Past Commander Post 50,

Ran this program for 25 years when I met him. He saw it as an activity for young men to enjoy. Winning and losing were the least of his concerns. His only goal was to have a team. Later became the 3rd District Baseball Chairman and served on the rules Committee for the Department of Indiana. He served as Baseball Chairman for 45 years. He died in 2002.

(Quote)…"I don't care who you beat, as long as you beat Post 357!"

Forest Miller - South Bend Tribune Sports Writer - Pencil in right hand, Note pad in left.

Ever astute and omnipresent at our tournament games.

He traveled with us through the state tournament and continued on to Chicago for the National Regional. He followed us at his own expense to the National Finals and let my wife and son ride with him. He wrote those stories as an independent by-line. Woody always knew about the upcoming teams. His mere presence in the press box made me feel a little more secure. He was a strong supporter of our team even though you couldn't sense it in his writing. Over the years we became close friends. Woody died on March 7, 2009

(Quote) ... "There isn't a team here that you can't beat!"

Appendix 2

AMERICAN LEGION BASEBALL PROGRAM

In 1977 George Rulon, the National Baseball Chairman, made a statement at the American Legion World Series banquet that ..."56% of current major leaguers had participated in American Legion baseball programs throughout the country." It is now estimated that since its inception in 1926 over two million boys have played American Legion Baseball. These numbers alone make American Legion Baseball a very important part of the American past time. The following facts will explain why it is so important in Indiana and in so many other parts of the country.

American Legion baseball is the epitome of neighborhood amateur baseball. It is steeped in fairness and even has a published Code of Sportsmanship. The National Program is run by a National Baseball Committee whose sole mission is to maintain the integrity of the program. Their only vested interest is to conduct the tournament and leave a legacy of a well run program. In South Bend, Indiana it is the step after high school programs and in most cases before college program participation. It has a year-end tournament that creates a venue for college and professional scouts to see players compete at highly competitive levels.

The attraction of this brand of baseball for me is this concept of taking your whole team into the tournament. The year end tournament is not an all-star tournament. The standing rules start with the fact that you can only draw players from a fixed area. You can recruit from a base high school and contiguous surrounding high schools up to a maximum enrollment level of 3600 students (current limits have changed). You have to submit a roster by July 1st and only those players on your official roster can play. No additional players can be added and only players who are enrolled or graduated from your list of high schools and are on your submitted roster are eligible to play in the tournament. In addition, players can't leave one team to play for another without a coach's signed release which is submitted to the state for approval. The state is the governing body that controls any exceptions.

The tournament is played using MLB National League rules which I also prefer over American League and high school rules. The games are nine innings, no designated hitter, no speed-up and no re-entry. The only variation from National League rules is the pitching rule which limits pitchers to twelve innings or three appearances in three calendar days, which is intended as a safety measure. The overall view of which I wasn't aware until after the tournament was over was that in 1977 we finished first out of approximately 3,800 American Legion teams from across the country.

The tournament structure made winning the American Legion National Championship no easy feat. It's double elimination in each of five separate tournaments levels. That means you have to lose two games in a level in order to be out of the tournament. This actually favors the stronger teams since it compensates for single game "upset" losses.

Although the tournament structure varies from state to state the rules for player recruitment, age limits and roster changes are the same nationally. In Indiana, the state tournament has three levels. The sectional is the first level with all of the local teams participating. The winners move on to the Regional Tournaments which quarter the state and the four Regional winners plus a host team, then play in the State Finals. Each level has the double elimination format.

Winning the State Championship gives your team the chance to participate in the National Tournament. This tournament is divided into two levels, the National Regional Tournaments and the National Finals, the World Series of American Legion Baseball. Again they are double elimination at both levels. There are eight sites for the National Regional Tournaments spread throughout the country. Sites are bid on and each is composed of six state champions plus a host team. The World Series participants are the eight National Regional tournament winners.

Most of the coaches in Indiana American Legion Baseball have been around for years and mirror the American Legion membership. They are true veterans of the baseball wars as the Legionnaires are veterans of military wars.

This format has been used for years and will continue to be used with only minor variations which have to be voted on and passed by the National Baseball Rules Committee. Now you know the American Legion Baseball program, the tournament structure and why I'm drawn to it.

The following code sets the tone for on-field deportment by players at all levels of American Legion Baseball tournaments.

THE CODE OF SPORTSMANSHIP

I will:
> Keep the rules
> Keep faith with my teammates
> Keep my temper
> Keep myself fit
> Keep a stout heart in defeat
> Keep my pride under in victory
> Keep a sound soul, a clean mind and a healthy body

Appendix 3

December 22, 1977

TO THE GRADUATES:

This was your last year with Post 50

The umpires' calls of our last game still echo in my ears. My thoughts are filled only by baseball; the cracks of bats and the thuds of baseballs hitting gloves. (You forgot to pick up the equipment the last game; but no matter, I retrieved it as a final chore that goes with the job. I'm used to doing it. I've done it on various fields all over the country.)

I'm wondering why I haven't given my personal items away. I guess in my heart I hope that in hoarding them, their presence will some -how inspire my own son to use them. The many uniforms I've collected hang lonely in my closet. As I travel, the ball diamonds which sprinkle the cities remind me of all the young people who have touched my life and made me richer for having known them.

I won't say good-bye, although somehow in this leave-taking there is a permanence which can't be removed. In future years I'll sit and reminisce with friends fighting back the lump in my throat, thinking of what we've shared and how you gave your all, for reasons which will become clear only later in your lives.

Seasons go faster with age -- March to August flies with ever-increasing speed. The sounds of baseball are muffled now. The visions are beginning to fog over. The excitement of the games, the defeats and the victories are becoming only vague memories.

A last reflection -- only you and I -- this is what will endure. My only hope is that somehow, through my attitudes, I have been able to convey to you, part of me.

With great affection.

Your friend and coach,

Mel Machuca

Authors' Biographies

WILL SHEPHERD makes his home in Warsaw, Indiana with son Peter, and daughter Emily. He teaches Health and coaches football at Warsaw Community High School. His baseball playing career ended following his graduation from Butler University in 1981.

Will coached high school baseball in Indiana for 20 years, 10 of those as the Head Coach at WCHS in Warsaw. Off the field, he enjoys fishing, reading, and playing cards. Born in South Bend in 1959, he grew up just south of town in LaPaz, Indiana.

Will played American Legion Baseball for South Bend Post 50 for three seasons from 1975-77. In that time he saw the program grow into a National Champion. Will, like his teammates, learned to play baseball *An Inning At A Time.*

MEL MACHUCA grew up in East Chicago, IN and is a member of South Bend Post 50. He and Lynda, his wife of 44 years, live in North Olmsted, OH near Cleveland. They have two grown sons; Todd who is married to Dana and Tait, an eligible bachelor, both graduated from Bowling Green State University.

A professional consultant with 38 years of experience in pharmaceutical sales and management, he believes in American Legion Baseball and has coached at this level for 23 years in four states. This year South Bend Post 50's accomplishment was included in the Indiana Baseball Hall of Fame. He also initiated a program to teach baseball fundamentals to 4-7 year olds entitled "Belly Button Basics" through the YMCA

"Managing a sales team and managing a baseball team have many common goals but the most important is developing people and teaching them to believe in themselves."

CPSIA information can be obtained at www.ICGtesting.com
Printed in the USA
LVOW101930140612

286096LV00002B/9/P